studysync®

Reading & Writing Companion

You and Me

How do relationships shape us?

studysync.com

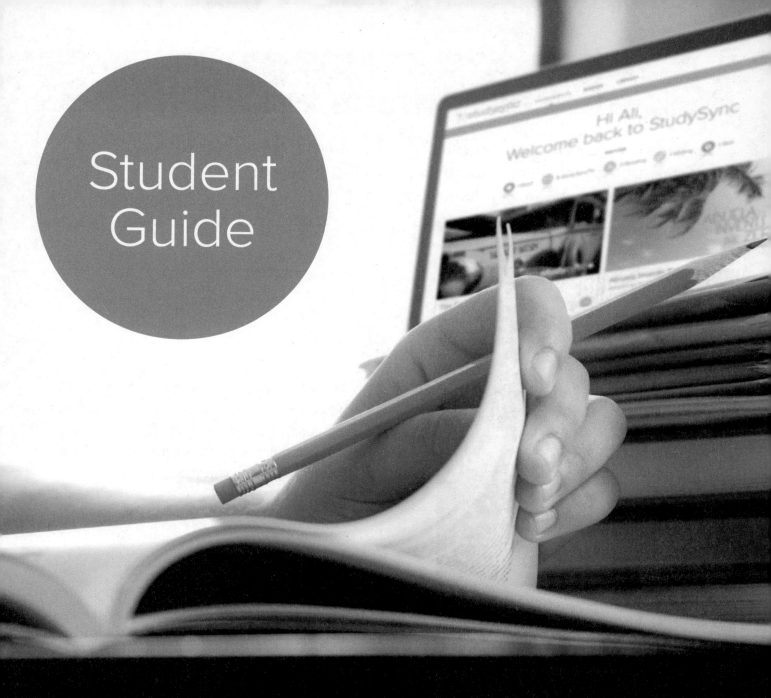

Student Guide

Getting Started

Welcome to the StudySync Reading & Writing Companion! In this book, you will find a collection of readings based on the theme of the unit you are studying. As you work through the readings, you will be asked to answer questions and perform a variety of tasks designed to help you closely analyze and understand each text selection. Read on for an explanation of each

Close Reading and Writing Routine

In each unit, you will read texts that share a common theme, despite their different genres, time periods, and authors. Each reading encourages a closer look through questions and a short writing assignment.

Eleven
FICTION
Sandra Cisneros
1991

Introduction

studysync●

Sandra Cisneros (b. 1954) is a renowned Chicana writer whose poems, novels, and short stories explore the complicated struggle of finding one's own identity. Cisneros is best known for her novel *The House on Mango Street* and the collection *Woman Hollering Creek and Other Stories*. "Eleven" is from the latter, the story of a girl named Rachel who experiences growing pains on her eleventh birthday. When her teacher insists that an ugly red sweater belongs to Rachel, the eleven-year-old has exceptional thoughts but can't share them. Even so, it's evident that the protagonist of Sandra Cisneros's short story has insight beyond her years.

Eleven

"You open your eyes and everything's
just like yesterday, only it's today.
And you don't feel eleven at all."

1. What they don't understand about birthdays and what they never tell you is that when you're eleven, you're also ten, and nine, and eight, and seven, and six, and five, and four, and three, and two, and one. And when you wake up on your eleventh birthday you expect to feel eleven, but you don't. You open your eyes and everything's just like yesterday, only it's today. And you don't feel eleven at all. You feel like you're still ten. And you are—underneath the year that makes you eleven.

2. Like some days you might say something stupid, and that's the part of you that's still ten. Or maybe some days you might need to sit on your mama's lap because you're scared, and that's the part of you that's five. And maybe one day when you're all grown up maybe you will need to cry like if you're three, and that's okay. That's what I tell Mama when she's sad and needs to cry. Maybe she's feeling three.

3. Because the way you grow old is kind of like an onion or like the rings inside a tree trunk or like my little wooden dolls that fit one inside the other, each year inside the next one. That's how being eleven years old is.

4. You don't feel eleven. Not right away. It takes a few days, weeks even, sometimes even months before you say Eleven when they ask you. And you don't feel smart eleven, not until you're almost twelve. That's the way it is.

5. Only today I wish I didn't have only eleven years rattling inside me like pennies in a tin Band-Aid box. Today I wish I was one hundred and two instead of eleven because if I was one hundred and two I'd have known what to say when Mrs. Price put the red sweater on my desk. I would've known how to tell her it wasn't mine instead of just sitting there with that look on my face and nothing coming out of my mouth.

6. "Whose is this?" Mrs. Price says, and she holds the red sweater up in the air for all the class to see. "Whose? It's been sitting in the coatroom for a month."

⊙ Skill: Figurative Language

The narrator uses similes when she compares aging to everyday things. When I picture onions, tree trunks, and wooden dolls, I notice they all have layers. She must mean that when you get older, you keep getting more layers.

① Introduction

An Introduction to each text provides historical context for your reading as well as information about the author. You will also learn about the genre of the text and the year in which it was written.

② Notes

Many times, while working through the activities after each text, you will be asked to **annotate** or **make annotations** about what you are reading. This means that you should highlight or underline words in the text and use the "Notes" column to make comments or jot down any questions you have. You may also want to note any unfamiliar vocabulary words here.

You will also see sample student annotations to go along with the Skill lesson for that text.

First Read

During your first reading of each selection, you should just try to get a general idea of the content and message of the reading. Don't worry if there are parts you don't understand or words that are unfamiliar to you. You'll have an opportunity later to dive deeper into the text.

Think Questions

These questions will ask you to start thinking critically about the text, asking specific questions about its purpose, and making connections to your prior knowledge and reading experiences. To answer these questions, you should go back to the text and draw upon specific evidence to support your responses. You will also begin to explore some of the more challenging vocabulary words in the selection.

Skills

Each Skill includes two parts: Checklist and Your Turn. In the Checklist, you will learn the process for analyzing the text. The model student annotations in the text provide examples of how you might make your own notes following the instructions in the Checklist. In the Your Turn, you will use those same instructions to practice the skill.

 Copyright © BookheadEd Learning, LLC

Right column panels

Eleven

 First Read

Read "Eleven." After you read, complete the Think Questions below.

THINK QUESTIONS

1. How does Rachel feel about the red sweater that is placed on her desk? Respond with textual evidence from the story as well as ideas that you have inferred from clues in the text.

2. According to Rachel, why does Sylvia say the sweater belongs to Rachel? Support your answer with textual evidence.

3. Write two or three sentences exploring why Mrs. Price responds as she does when Phyllis claims the sweater. Support your answer with textual evidence.

4. Find the word **raggedy** in paragraph 9 of "Eleven." Use context clues in the surrounding sentences, as well as the sentence in which the word appears, to determine the word's meaning. Write your definition here and identify clues that helped you figure out its meaning.

5. Use context clues to determine the meaning of **nonsense** as it is used in paragraph 15 of "Eleven." Write your definition here and identify clues that helped you figure out its meaning. Then check the meaning in a dictionary.

Eleven

 Skill:
Figurative Language

Use the Checklist to analyze Figurative Language in "Eleven." Refer to the sample student annotations about Figurative Language in the text.

CHECKLIST FOR FIGURATIVE LANGUAGE

To determine the meaning of figures of speech in a text, note the following:

✓ words that mean one thing literally and suggest something else

✓ similes, such as "strong as an ox"

✓ metaphors, such as "her eyes were stars"

✓ personification, such as "the daisies danced in the wind"

In order to interpret the meaning of a figure of speech in context, ask the following questions:

✓ Does any of the descriptive language in the text compare two seemingly unlike things?

✓ Do any descriptions include "like" or "as" that indicate a simile?

✓ Is there a direct comparison that suggests a metaphor?

✓ is a human quality is being used to describe this animal, object, force of nature or idea that suggests personification?

✓ How does the use of this figure of speech change your understanding of the thing or person being described?

YOUR TURN

1. How does the figurative language in paragraph 18 help readers understand Rachel's reaction to the sweater?

○ A. The metaphors in the paragraph help readers understand how uncomfortable Rachel feels in the sweater.

○ B. The similes in the paragraph help readers understand how uncomfortable Rachel feels in the sweater.

○ C. The metaphors in the paragraph make it clear to readers that Rachel is overreacting about the sweater.

○ D. The similes in the paragraph make it clear to readers that Rachel is overreacting about the sweater.

2. How does the figurative language in paragraph 19 help readers visualize Rachel's behavior?

○ A. The mention of "little animal noises" tells readers that Rachel is acting more like an animal than a human.

○ B. The metaphor of "clown-sweater arms" shows that Rachel is able to see the humorous side in her experience.

○ C. The similes about her body shaking "like when you have the hiccups" and her head hurting "like when you drink milk too fast" connect to unpleasant experiences most readers have had.

○ D. The statement that "there aren't any more tears left in [her] eyes" suggests that Rachel is starting to calm down.

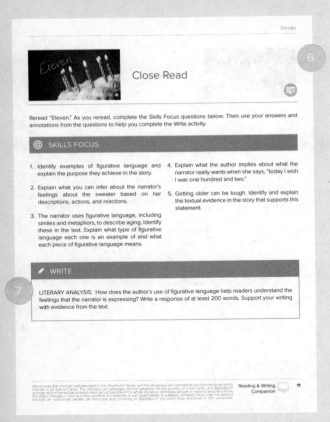

Eleven

Close Read

Reread "Eleven." As you reread, complete the Skills Focus questions below. Then use your answers and annotations from the questions to help you complete the Write activity.

◎ SKILLS FOCUS

1. Identify examples of figurative language and explain the purpose they achieve in the story.

2. Explain what you can infer about the narrator's feelings about the sweater based on her descriptions, actions, and reactions.

3. The narrator uses figurative language, including similes and metaphors, to describe aging. Identify these in the text. Explain what type of figurative language each one is an example of and what each piece of figurative language means.

4. Explain what the author implies about what the narrator really wants when she says, "today I wish I was one hundred and two."

5. Getting older can be tough. Identify and explain the textual evidence in the story that supports this statement.

✏ WRITE

LITERARY ANALYSIS: How does the author's use of figurative language help readers understand the feelings that the narrator is expressing? Write a response of at least 200 words. Support your writing with evidence from the text.

Close Read & Skills Focus

After you have completed the First Read, you will be asked to go back and read the text more closely and critically. Before you begin your Close Read, you should read through the Skills Focus to get an idea of the concepts you will want to focus on during your second reading. You should work through the Skills Focus by making annotations, highlighting important concepts, and writing notes or questions in the "Notes" column. Depending on instructions from your teacher, you may need to respond online or use a separate piece of paper to start expanding on your thoughts and ideas.

Write

Your study of each selection will end with a writing assignment. For this assignment, you should use your notes, annotations, personal ideas, and answers to both the Think and Skills Focus questions. Be sure to read the prompt carefully and address each part of it in your writing.

English Language Learner

The English Language Learner texts focus on improving language proficiency. You will practice learning strategies and skills in individual and group activities to become better readers, writers, and speakers.

Lost Island

FICTION

Introduction

Marina wakes up alone, thirsty, and hungry on a deserted island. How did she get here, and why is her head throbbing? As she slowly recalls a large wave smashing into Uncle Merlin's fishing boat, Marina takes her first steps towards survival.

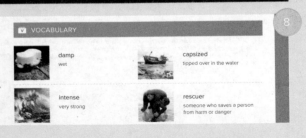

ⓥ VOCABULARY

damp
wet

capsized
tipped over in the water

intense
very strong

rescuer
someone who saves a person from harm or danger

Extended Writing Project and Grammar

This is your opportunity to use genre characteristics and craft to compose meaningful, longer written works exploring the theme of each unit. You will draw information from your readings, research, and own life experiences to complete the assignment.

1 Writing Project

After you have read all of the unit text selections, you will move on to a writing project. Each project will guide you through the process of writing your essay. Student models will provide guidance and help you organize your thoughts. One unit ends with an **Extended Oral Project**, which will give you an opportunity to develop your oral language and communication skills.

2 Writing Process Steps

There are four steps in the writing process: Plan, Draft, Revise, and Edit and Publish. During each step, you will form and shape your writing project, and each lesson's peer review will give you the chance to receive feedback from your peers and teacher.

3 Writing Skills

Each Skill lesson focuses on a specific strategy or technique that you will use during your writing project. Each lesson presents a process for applying the skill to your own work and gives you the opportunity to practice it to improve your writing.

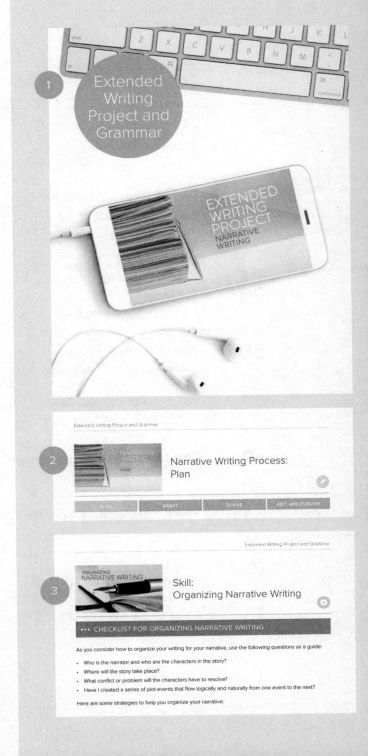

You and Me

How do relationships shape us?

Genre Focus: **POETRY**

Texts

 Paired Readings

Extended Writing Project and Grammar

Unit 2: You and Me
How do relationships shape us?

SHARON CREECH

In a suburb of Cleveland, Ohio, Sharon Creech (b. 1945) grew up in a house filled with visiting relatives and friends, along with her parents, sister, and three brothers. Each summer, Creech's parents would pile all five children into the family car to go on a long road trip. On one of these trips, when Creech was twelve years old, they went to Idaho, and that experience became the basis of the story told in the novel *Walk Two Moons* (1994).

COUNTEE CULLEN

In 1918, at the age of fifteen, Countee Cullen (1903-1946) lost the woman who cared for him: his grandmother. His new guardian would be the pastor of Salem Methodist Episcopal Church, which hosted the largest congregation in Harlem. Cullen's poetry is regarded as a significant voice of the Harlem Renaissance, a vibrant period that ushered in an innovative generation of African American writers in New York City. Cullen often expressed that he believed art could transcend race, and hoped his poems would bring together people from all walks of life.

NIKKI GIOVANNI

Nikki Giovanni (b. 1943) is an African American poet who grew up during the civil rights movement and launched her career at the age of twenty-five with her collection of poems, *Black Feeling Black Talk* (1968), published shortly after the assassination of Dr. Martin Luther King Jr. Around the same time, Giovanni was a preeminent author in the Black Arts Movement and was friends with Rosa Parks and Muhammad Ali. She went on to develop a distinguished career as a poet and activist, and is currently a college professor in Virginia.

FRANCISCO JIMÉNEZ

Francisco Jiménez (b. 1943) is a Chicano writer of fiction and memoir who moved from his home in Mexico to California and back several times before he reached adulthood. Along with his family, Jiménez was a migrant field-worker, moving through California to pick crops: Corcoran for cotton, Santa Maria for strawberries, and Fresno for grapes. Despite facing many hardships, including not having a permanent home or consistent education, Jiménez excelled in school and went on to become a college professor and a successful author.

JACKI JING

NCAA Division I athlete Jacki Jing (b. 1986) grew up playing volleyball in Centennial, Colorado. She received a full athletic scholarship to the State University of New York at Binghamton, where she earned degrees in political science and English, and was later inducted into their Athletic Hall of Fame in 2014. Jing went on to become a television journalist, reporting and anchoring for stations in Colorado, New York, Massachusetts, and Louisiana.

DAVID KHERDIAN

"What we learn in childhood is carved in stone. What we learn as adults is carved in ice," writes David Kherdian (b. 1931). The poet, biographer, and editor was born to two survivors of the Armenian Genocide and raised in Wisconsin near Root River. He excelled at sports, especially basketball, football, and softball, and also loved to read and draw. From an early age, he was exposed to and fought against the discrimination he experienced as a child of immigrants.

WALTER DEAN MYERS

Walter Dean Myers (1937–2004) was raised in Harlem by his adopted family. As a child, he was a gifted student and athlete but was teased for having a speech impediment and was known to have a quick temper. He found solace in reading and writing, and would grow up to become an award-winning author of books for young adults and children. His first book, *Where Does the Day Go* (1969), was written for a contest for African American writers, and marked the start of a career-long mission to write literature for and about people of color.

MILDRED TAYLOR

Mildred Taylor (b. 1943) moved with her family from Jackson, Mississippi, to newly-integrated Toledo, Ohio, when she was only three months old. She describes herself as a quiet child in a family of prodigious storytellers. The family visited Mississippi every year, where her great-grandfather had purchased land in the late 1800s that the family still owns. Taylor used those visits to the American South and family lore as the basis for her stories. *Roll of Thunder, Hear My Cry*, the second novel of the saga, won the 1977 Newbery Award.

HOLLY WARLICK

When Holly Warlick (b. 1958) was named head coach of the University of Tennessee's women's basketball team, her predecessor Pat Summitt admitted that Warlick had already been leading the team in her role as assistant coach. The legendary Summitt passed her whistle to Warlick after receiving a diagnosis of Alzheimer's Disease in 2011. Warlick was formerly a player on Summitt's team, and was the first player in Tennessee sports history to have her jersey retired at the end of her playing career.

PAT MORA

Mexican American author Pat Mora (b. 1942) grew up surrounded by books in El Paso, Texas, and fell in love with reading and writing at an early age. Her poetry and stories explore Chicana identity in the region of the border and are written in both English and Spanish. Mora grew up with bilingual parents and says that switching between English and Spanish was the rhythm of her childhood. She went on to replicate a book-loving, bilingual home for her own three children.

Walk Two Moons

FICTION
Sharon Creech
1994

Introduction

On a trip with her grandparents, Salamanca, or Sal, tells them the story of her best friend, Phoebe Winterbottom. Sal met Phoebe when she and her father left their farm in Kentucky and moved to Ohio, where Margaret Cadaver lives. Sal's father befriended Margaret after her mother disappeared. Phoebe is certain that Mrs. Cadaver, who lives next door to her family, is somehow sinister, and is responsible for the strange notes that appear on her family's doorstep. They wind up having a magical effect on the grief that surrounds Phoebe's mother, and help Sal understand her own identity. A beloved classic, this novel by Sharon Creech (b. 1945) has won numerous awards, including the Newbery Medal.

"In the course of a lifetime, what does it matter?"

Copyright © BookheadEd Learning, LLC

1   A few days after Phoebe and I had seen Mr. Birkway and Mrs. Cadaver whacking away at the rhododendron, I walked home with Phoebe after school. She was as **crotchety** and **sullen** as a three-legged mule, and I was not quite sure why. She had been asking me why I had not said anything to my father about Mrs. Cadaver and Mr. Birkway, and I told her that I was waiting for the right time.

2   "Your father was over there yesterday," Phoebe said. "I saw him. He'd better watch out. What would you do if Mrs. Cadaver chopped up your father? Would you go live with your mother?"

3   It surprised me when she said that, reminding me that I had told Phoebe nothing about my mother. "Yes, I suppose I would go live with her." That was impossible and I knew it, but for some reason I could not tell Phoebe that, so I lied.

4   Phoebe's mother was sitting at the kitchen table when we walked in. In front of her was a pan of burned brownies. She blew her nose. "Oh sweetie," she said, "you startled me. How was it?"

5   "How was what?" Phoebe asked.

6   "Why, sweetie, school of course. How was it? How were your classes?"

7   "Okay."

8   "Just okay?" Mrs. Winterbottom suddenly leaned over and kissed Phoebe's cheek.

9   "I'm not a baby, you know," Phoebe said, wiping off the kiss.

10 Mrs. Winterbottom stabbed the brownies with a knife. "Want one?" she asked.

11 "They're burned," Phoebe said. "Besides, I'm fat."

NOTES

Skill: Language, Style, and Audience

The author chooses words like sullen *to show the audience that Sal is smart because this is not a word kids often use. After reading this paragraph, I also know that Sal is from the country because she mentions a mule. She's funny, and she's tolerant because she doesn't get mad that Phoebe is grouchy.*

NOTES

12 "Oh sweetie, you're not fat," Mrs. Winterbottom said.

13 "I am."

14 "No, you're not."

15 "I am, I am, I am!" Phoebe shouted at her mother. "You don't have to bake things for me. I'm too fat. And you don't have to wait here for me to come home. I'm thirteen now."

16 Phoebe marched upstairs. Mrs. Winterbottom offered me a brownie, so I sat down at the table. What I started doing was remembering the day before my mother left. I did not know it was to be her last day home. Several times that day, my mother asked me if I wanted to walk up in the fields with her. It was drizzling outside, and I was cleaning out my desk, and I just did not feel like going. "Maybe later," I kept saying. When she asked me for about the tenth time, I said, "No! I don't want to go. Why do you keep asking me?" I don't know why I did that. I didn't mean anything by it, but that was one of the last memories she had of me, and I wished I could take it back.

17 Phoebe's sister, Prudence, stormed into the house, slamming the door behind her. "I blew it. I just know it!" she wailed.

18 "Oh sweetie," her mother said.

19 "I did!" Prudence said. "I did, I did, I did."

Skill: Textual Evidence

Using textual evidence, I can make inferences about Mrs. Winterbottom's sadness. I think Mrs. Winterbottom and Prudence have a rocky relationship. I can also infer Sal's guilt for how she treated her mother on their last day together.

20 Mrs. Winterbottom half-heartedly chipped away at the burned brownies and asked Prudence if she would have another chance at cheerleading **tryouts.**

21 "Yes, tomorrow. But I know I'm going to blow it!"

22 Her mother said, "Maybe I'll come along and watch." I could tell that Mrs. Winterbottom was trying to rise above some awful sadness she was feeling, but Prudence couldn't see that. Prudence had her own **agenda**, just as I had had my own agenda that day my mother wanted me to walk with her. I couldn't see my own mother's sadness.

23 "What?" Prudence said. "Come along and *watch*?"

24 "Yes, wouldn't that be nice?"

25 "No!" Prudence said. "No, no, no. You can't. It would be awful."

26 I heard the front door open and shut and Phoebe came in the kitchen waving a white envelope. "Guess what was on the steps?" she said.

27   Mrs. Winterbottom took the envelope and turned it over and over before she slowly unsealed it and slipped out the message.

28   "Oh," she said. "Who is doing this?" She held out the piece of paper: *In the course of a lifetime, what does it matter?*

29   Prudence said, "Well, I have more important things to worry about, I can **assure** you. I know I'm going to blow those cheerleading tryouts, I just know it."

30   On and on she went, until Phoebe said, "Cripes, Prudence, in the course of a lifetime, what does it matter?"

31   At that moment, it was as if a switch went off in Mrs. Winterbottom's brain. She put her hand to her mouth and stared out the window. She was invisible to Prudence and Phoebe, though. They did not notice.

32   Phoebe said, "Are these cheerleading tryouts such a big deal? Will you even remember them in five years?"

33   "Yes!" Prudence said. "Yes, I most certainly will."

34   "How about ten years? Will you remember them in ten?"

35   "Yes!" Prudence said.

36   As I walked home, I thought about the message. *In the course of a lifetime, what does it matter?* I said it over and over. I wondered about the mysterious messenger, and I wondered about all the things in the course of a lifetime that would not matter. I did not think cheerleading tryouts would matter, but I was not so sure about yelling at your mother. I was certain, however, that if your mother left, it would be something that mattered in the whole long course of your lifetime.

Excerpted from *Walk Two Moons* by Sharon Creech, published by HarperCollins Publishers.

Please note that excerpts and passages in the StudySync® library and this workbook are intended as touchstones to generate interest in an author's work. The excerpts and passages do not substitute for the reading of entire texts, and StudySync® strongly recommends that students seek out and purchase the whole literary or informational work in order to experience it as the author intended. Links to online resellers are available in our digital library. In addition, complete works may be ordered through an authorized reseller by filling out and returning to StudySync® the order form enclosed in this workbook.

Reading & Writing Companion

3

First Read

Read *Walk Two Moons*. After you read, complete the Think Questions below.

☁ THINK QUESTIONS

1. What kind of relationship does Mrs. Winterbottom have with her daughters Prudence and Phoebe? Cite evidence from the text to support your answer.

2. What message does Phoebe find on the steps? What effect does it have on the narrator? Be sure to cite textual evidence to support your answer.

3. Mood is the emotional quality or atmosphere of a story. What is the mood in Mrs. Winterbottom's kitchen in this excerpt from *Walk Two Moons*? Which words and descriptions contribute to this mood?

4. Find the word **agenda** in paragraph 22 of *Walk Two Moons*. Use context clues in the surrounding sentences, as well as the sentence in which the word appears, to determine the word's meaning. Write your definition here and identify clues that helped you figure out its meaning.

5. Use context clues to determine the meaning of **assure** as it is used in paragraph 29 of *Walk Two Moons*. Write your definition here and identify clues that helped you figure out its meaning. Then check the meaning in a dictionary.

Skill:
Language, Style, and Audience

Use the Checklist to analyze Language, Style, and Audience in *Walk Two Moons*. Refer to the sample student annotations about Language, Style, and Audience in the text.

••• CHECKLIST FOR LANGUAGE, STYLE, AND AUDIENCE

In order to determine an author's style, do the following:

- ✓ identify and define any unfamiliar words or phrases

- ✓ use context, including the meaning of surrounding words and phrases

- ✓ note specific words and phrases that the author uses to create a response in the reader

- ✓ note the tone that the author is communicating through the word choices

To analyze the impact of specific word choice on meaning and tone, ask the following questions:

- ✓ How did the language impact your understanding of the meaning of the text?

- ✓ What stylistic choices can you identify in the text? How does the style influence your understanding of the language?

- ✓ How could various audiences interpret this language? What different possible emotional responses can you list?

- ✓ How does the writer's choice of words impact or create a specific tone in the text?

Please note that excerpts and passages in the StudySync® library and this workbook are intended as touchstones to generate interest in an author's work. The excerpts and passages do not substitute for the reading of entire texts, and StudySync® strongly recommends that students seek out and purchase the whole literary or informational work in order to experience it as the author intended. Links to online resellers are available in our digital library. In addition, complete works may be ordered through an authorized reseller by filling out and returning to StudySync® the order form enclosed in this workbook.

Reading & Writing
Companion

5

Skill:
Language, Style, And Audience

Reread paragraphs 17–25 of *Walk Two Moons*. Then, using the Checklist on the previous page, answer the multiple-choice questions below.

⟳ YOUR TURN

1. How does the author use the words *stormed* and *wailed* in paragraph 17 to characterize Prudence?

   ○ A. Prudence is dramatic and self-absorbed.
   ○ B. Prudence is quiet and respectful.
   ○ C. Prudence is loud, but interested in others.
   ○ D. Prudence is distracted, but caring.

2. What does the author's repetition of words in paragraphs 19 and 25 reveal about Prudence?

   ○ A. Prudence wants to make sure she's being heard.
   ○ B. Prudence accommodates her mother's poor hearing.
   ○ C. Prudence is childish, and she throws tantrums.
   ○ D. Prudence is a good speaker, and she emphasizes her points.

3. What is the effect of the author's use of italics in paragraph 23?

   ○ A. The italics show gratitude in Prudence's tone.
   ○ B. The italics show horror in Prudence's tone.
   ○ C. The italics show humor in Prudence's tone.
   ○ D. The italics show sorrow in Prudence's tone.

Skill:
Textual Evidence

Use the Checklist to analyze Textual Evidence in *Walk Two Moons*. Refer to the sample student annotations about Textual Evidence in the text.

••• CHECKLIST FOR TEXTUAL EVIDENCE

In order to support analysis and ideas by citing textual evidence that is explicitly stated in the text, do the following:

- ✓ read the text closely and critically

- ✓ identify what the text says explicitly

- ✓ find the most relevant textual evidence that supports your analysis and ideas

- ✓ consider why an author explicitly states specific details and information

- ✓ cite the specific words, phrases, sentences, or paragraphs from the text that support your analysis and ideas

In order to interpret implicit meanings in a text by making inferences, do the following:

- ✓ combine information directly stated in the text with your own knowledge, experiences, and observations

- ✓ cite the specific words, phrases, sentences, or paragraphs from the text that support these inferences

In order to cite textual evidence to support an analysis of what the text says explicitly as well as inferences drawn from the text, consider the following questions:

- ✓ Have I read the text closely and critically?

- ✓ What inferences am I making about the text? What textual evidence am I using to support these inferences?

- ✓ Am I quoting the evidence from the text correctly?

- ✓ Does my textual evidence logically relate to my analysis?

Skill:
Textual Evidence

Reread paragraphs 27–36 of *Walk Two Moons*. Then, using the Checklist on the previous page, answer the multiple-choice questions below.

⟳ YOUR TURN

1. What evidence explicitly stated in the text best describes Prudence's reaction to the letter?

   ○ A. "'Cripes, Prudence, in the course of a lifetime, what does it matter?'"
   ○ B. "'Well, I have more important things to worry about, I can assure you.'"
   ○ C. "She put her hand to her mouth and stared out the window."
   ○ D. "I wondered about all the things in the course of a lifetime that would not matter."

2. In paragraph 31, what is the effect of the letter on Mrs. Winterbottom, and how is this effect revealed by the author?

   ○ A. Mrs. Winterbottom continues to be confused by the letter, which the author reveals by having Mrs. Winterbottom put her hand to her mouth.
   ○ B. Mrs. Winterbottom doesn't show interest in the letter, which the author reveals with the narration that Mrs. Winterbottom stares out the window.
   ○ C. Mrs. Winterbottom suddenly figures something out about the letter, which the author reveals with the narration that a switch went off in Mrs. Winterbottom's brain.
   ○ D. Mrs. Winterbottom opens the letter and disappears from the kitchen, which the author reveals with the narration that Mrs. Winterbottom is invisible to her daughters.

3. Which message can be inferred from this scene of *Walk Two Moons*?

   ○ A. The past and the present remain separate time periods in one's life.
   ○ B. The present is more important than the past.
   ○ C. The past can invade the present through triggered memories.
   ○ D. Past events determine future events through present choices.

 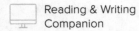

Close Read

Reread *Walk Two Moons*. As you reread, complete the Skills Focus questions below. Then use your answers and annotations from the questions to help you complete the Write activity.

◎ SKILLS FOCUS

1. Identify evidence that shows how the author contrasts Sal's treatment of her own mother with the way Phoebe and Prudence respond to their mother, Mrs. Winterbottom.

2. Identify evidence that shows what Sal learns about herself after witnessing the scene between Mrs. Winterbottom, Phoebe, and Prudence.

3. Phoebe finds a note on the doorstep that asks, "In the course of a lifetime, what does it matter?" What inference can you draw from the text to explain Mrs. Winterbottom's reaction to the note? What evidence explicitly stated in the text explains Prudence's reaction?

4. Explain how the author's word choice influenced the reader's understanding of the characters of Phoebe and Mrs. Winterbottom.

5. Identify evidence in the last paragraph that reveals what Sal realizes when she reflects back about her own mother leaving home.

✏ WRITE

NARRATIVE: Rewrite this excerpt from *Walk Two Moons* with Phoebe, Prudence, or Mrs. Winterbottom as the narrator instead of Sal. Use evidence explicitly stated in the text, as well as inferences drawn from the text, to identify the narrator's relationship with the other characters. In your narrative, select language that reflects an appropriate tone for the narrator you choose.

Roll of Thunder, Hear My Cry

FICTION
Mildred D. Taylor
1976

Introduction

Written by Mildred D. Taylor (b. 1943), *Roll of Thunder, Hear My Cry* is the gripping story of the Logans, a land-owning black family in the Deep South struggling to keep things together during a tumultuous year in the 1930s. Largely insulated from the injustices of the world around her, but raised with a strong sense of fairness, nine-year-old Cassie is only beginning to understand the realities of racism and the everyday terror it brings to the grown-ups in her community. In the excerpt here, neighbors bring bad news for her father. Published in 1976, Taylor's novel won the Newbery Medal the following year.

"We keep doing what we gotta, and we don't give up. We can't. . . ."

1   When supper was ready, I eagerly grabbed the iron bell before Christopher-John or Little Man could claim it, and ran onto the back porch to summon Papa, Mr. Morrison, and Stacey from the fields. As the three of them washed up on the back porch, Mama went to the end of the porch where Papa stood alone. "What did Mr. Jamison want?" she asked, her voice barely **audible.**

2   Papa took the towel Mama handed him, but did not reply immediately. I was just inside the kitchen dipping out the butter beans. I moved closer to the window so that I could hear his answer.

3   "Don't keep anything from me, David. If there's trouble, I want to know."

4   Papa looked down at her. "Nothing to worry 'bout, honey . . . . just seems that Thurston Wallace been in town talking 'bout how he's not gonna let a few smart colored folks ruin his business. Says he's gonna put a stop to this shopping in Vicksburg. That's all."

5   Mama sighed and stared out across the plowed field to the sloping pasture land. "I'm feeling scared, David," she said.

6   Papa put down the towel. "Not yet, Mary. It's not time to be scared yet. They're just talking."

7   Mama turned and faced him. "And when they stop talking?"

8   "Then . . . then maybe it'll be time. But right now, pretty lady," he said, leading her by the hand toward the kitchen door, "right now I've got better things to think about."

NOTES

Skill:
Story Structure

I see that Mama is nervous because the narrator can hardly hear her ask the question about Mr. Jamison. This seems to be part of the conflict.

Papa does not seem worried about the situation with Mr. Jamison, but the problem seems serious. How will the family solve this problem?

Please note that excerpts and passages in the StudySync® library and this workbook are intended as touchstones to generate interest in an author's work. The excerpts and passages do not substitute for the reading of entire texts, and StudySync® strongly recommends that students seek out and purchase the whole literary or informational work in order to experience it as the author intended. Links to online resellers are available in our digital library. In addition, complete works may be ordered through an authorized reseller by filling out and returning to StudySync® the order form enclosed in this workbook.

Reading & Writing Companion   **11**

Skill: Connotation and Denotation

I am not sure what this word means, but I can tell that Papa is very happy because he seems excited about the dinner. In this context, it seems like he is looking down at the table because he sees the dinner as he comes into the room. I think the word beamed means that he has a big smile on his face because he is very happy about seeing the dinner.

Skill: Theme

Mama is still scared and anxious, but Cassie hopes for a solution. This hope starts to go away though, which can be seen by the way her words keep getting interrupted. Her desperation and Mama's fear show the theme: fear can make people lose hope even though they try not to.

9 Quickly I poured the rest of the butter beans into the bowl and hurried across the kitchen to the table. As Mama and Papa entered, I slid onto the bench beside Little Man and Christopher-John. Papa beamed down at the table.

10 "Well, look-a-here!" he exclaimed. "Good ole butter beans and cornbread! You better come on, Mr. Morrison! You too, son!" he called. "These womenfolks done gone and fixed us a feast."

11 After school was out, spring drooped quickly toward summer; yet Papa had not left for the railroad. He seemed to be waiting for something, and I secretly hoped that whatever that something was, it would never come so that he would not leave. But one evening as he, Mama, Big Ma, Mr. Morrison, and Stacey sat on the front porch while Christopher-John, Little Man, and I dashed around the yard chasing fireflies, I overheard him say, "Sunday I'm gonna have to go. Don't want to though. I got this gut feeling it ain't over yet. It's too easy."

12 I released the firefly **imprisoned** in my hand and sat beside Papa and Stacey on the steps. "Papa, please," I said, leaning against his leg, "don't go this year." Stacey looked out into the falling night, his face resigned, and said nothing.

13 Papa put out his large hand and caressed my face. "Got to, Cassie girl," he said softly. "Baby, there's bills to pay and ain't no money coming in. Your mama's got no job come fall and there's the **mortgage** and next year's taxes to think of."

14 "But, Papa, we planted more cotton this year. Won't that pay the taxes?"

15 Papa shook his head. "With Mr. Morrison here we was able to plant more, but that cotton is for living on; the railroad money is for the taxes and the mortgage."

16 I looked back at Mama wanting her to speak, to persuade him to stay, but when I saw her face I knew that she would not. She had known he would leave, just as we all had known.

17 "Papa, just another week or two, couldn't you—"

18 "I can't, baby. May have lost my job already."

19 "But Papa—"

20 "Cassie, that's enough now," Mama said from the deepening shadows.

NOTES

21 I grew quiet and Papa put his arms around Stacey and me, his hands falling casually over our shoulders. From the edge of the lawn where Little Man and Christopher-John had **ventured** after lightning bugs, Little Man called, "Somebody's coming!" A few minutes later Mr. Avery and Mr. Lanier emerged from the dusk and walked up the sloping lawn. Mama sent Stacey and me to get more chairs for the porch, then we settled back beside Papa still sitting on the steps, his back propped against a pillar facing the visitors.

22 "You goin' up to the store tomorrow, David?" Mr. Avery asked after all the amenities had been said. Since the first trip in January, Mr. Morrison had made one other trip to Vicksburg, but Papa had not gone with him.

23 Papa motioned to Mr. Morrison. "Mr. Morrison and me going the day after tomorrow. Your wife brought down that list of things you need yesterday."

24 Mr. Avery cleared his throat nervously. "It's—it's that list I come 'bout, David. . . . I don't want them things no more."

25 The porch grew silent.

26 When no one said anything, Mr. Avery glanced at Mr. Lanier, and Mr. Lanier shook his head and continued. "Mr. Granger making it hard on us, David. Said we gonna have to give him sixty percent of the cotton, 'stead of fifty . . . now that the cotton's planted and it's too late to plant more. . . . Don't s'pose though that it makes much difference. The way cotton sells these days, seems the more we plant, the less money we gets anyways—"

27 Mr. Avery's coughing interrupted him and he waited patiently until the coughing had stopped before he went on. "I'm gonna be hard put to pay that debt in Vicksburg, David, but I'm gonna. . . . I want you to know that."

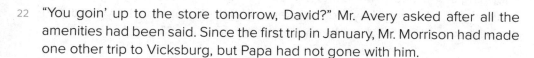

28 Mr. Avery's coughing started again and for a while there was only the coughing and the silence. But when the coughing ceased, Mr. Lanier said, "I pray to God there was a way we could stay in this thing, but we can't go on no chain gang, David."

29 Papa nodded. "Don't expect you to, Silas."

30 Mr. Avery laughed softly. "We sure had 'em goin' for a time though, didn't we?"

31 "Yes," agreed Papa quietly, "we sure did."

32 When the men had left, Stacey snapped, "They got no right pulling out! Just 'cause them Wallaces threaten them one time they go jumping all over themselves to get out like a bunch of scared jackrabbits—"

33 Papa stood suddenly and grabbed Stacey upward. "You, boy, don't you get so grown you go to talking 'bout more than you know. Them men, they doing what they've gotta do. You got any idea what a risk they took just to go shopping in Vicksburg in the first place? They go on that chain gang and their families got nothing. They'll get kicked off that plot of land they tend and there'll be no place for them to go. You understand that?"

34 "Y-yessir," said Stacey. Papa released him and stared moodily into the night. "You were born blessed, boy, with land of your own. If you hadn't been, you'd cry out for it while you try to survive . . . like Mr. Lanier and Mr. Avery. Maybe even do what they doing now. It's hard on a man to give up, but sometimes it seems there just ain't nothing else he can do."

35 "I . . . I'm sorry, Papa," Stacey muttered.

36 After a moment, Papa reached out and draped his arm over Stacey's shoulder.

37 "Papa," I said, standing to join them, "we giving up too?"

38 Papa looked down at me and brought me closer, then waved his hand toward the drive. "You see that fig tree over yonder, Cassie? Them other trees all around . . . that oak and walnut, they're a lot bigger and they take up more room and give so much shade they almost **overshadow** that little ole fig. But that fig tree's got roots that run deep, and it belongs in that yard as much as that oak and walnut. It keeps on blooming, bearing good fruit year after year, knowing all the time it'll never get as big as them other trees. Just keeps on growing and doing what it gotta do. It don't give up. It give up, it'll die. There's a lesson to be learned from that little tree, Cassie girl, 'cause we're like it. We keep doing what we gotta, and we don't give up. We can't."

Excerpted from Roll of Thunder, Hear My Cry by Mildred D. Taylor, published by Puffin Books.

First Read

Read *Roll of Thunder, Hear My Cry*. After you read, complete the Think Questions below.

☁ THINK QUESTIONS

1. Why are Thurston Wallace and Mr. Granger angry with the black farmers? Cite textual evidence from the selection to support your answer.

2. Write two or three sentences describing why Papa is in a better position than Mr. Avery and Mr. Lanier to stand up to Thurston Wallace. Cite textual evidence from the selection to support your answer.

3. Voice is the use of language that conveys the distinctive personality of the writer or speaker, the narrator, or a particular character. In paragraph 33, what words or phrases does Papa use when talking with Stacey that give you a sense of his personality? How would you describe his personality? Cite textual evidence from the selection to support your answer.

4. Find the word **imprisoned** in paragraph 12 of *Roll of Thunder, Hear My Cry*. Use context clues in the surrounding sentences, as well as the sentence in which the word appears, to determine the word's meaning. Write your definition here and identify clues that helped you figure out its meaning.

5. Use context to determine the meaning of the word **ventured** as it is used in *Roll of Thunder, Hear My Cry* in paragraph 21. Write your definition here and identify clues that helped you figure out its meaning. Then check the meaning in a dictionary.

Skill:
Connotation and Denotation

Use the Checklist to analyze Connotation and Denotation in *Roll of Thunder, Hear My Cry.* Refer to the sample student annotations about Connotation and Denotation in the text.

••• CHECKLIST FOR CONNOTATION AND DENOTATION

In order to identify the denotative meanings of words and phrases, use the following steps:

✓ first, note unfamiliar words and phrases; key words used to describe important characters, events, and ideas; or words that inspire an emotional reaction

✓ next, verify the denotative meaning of words by consulting a reference material such as a dictionary, glossary, or thesaurus

To better understand the meaning of words and phrases as they are used in a text, including connotative meanings, use the following questions:

✓ What is the genre or subject of the text? How does that affect the possible meaning of a word or phrase?

✓ Does the word create a positive, negative, or neutral emotion?

✓ What synonyms or alternative phrasing help you describe the connotative meaning of the word?

To determine the meaning of words and phrases as they are used in a text, including connotative meanings, use the following questions:

✓ What is the meaning of the word or phrase? What is the connotation as well as the denotation?

✓ If I substitute a synonym based on denotation, is the meaning the same? How does it change the meaning of the text?

Skill:
Connotation and Denotation

Reread paragraph 21 of *Roll of Thunder, Hear My Cry*. Then, using the Checklist on the previous page, answer the multiple-choice questions below.

⟳ YOUR TURN

1. This question has two parts. First, answer Part A. Then, answer Part B.

   Part A: What is the denotative meaning of the word **ventured** as it is used in the context of paragraph 21?

   ○ A. set out
   ○ B. yelled loudly
   ○ C. remembered
   ○ D. caught

   Part B: Based on your answer to Part A, what is the intended connotation of the word *venture* below? Which definition BEST supports the conclusion drawn in Part A?

   ○ A. Positive - the boys are having fun venturing out after the bugs.
   ○ B. Negative - the boys are afraid to go after the bugs.
   ○ C. Negative - the boys are sad about hunting the bugs.
   ○ D. Neither positive nor negative - the boys have no feelings about chasing the bugs.

Skill: Theme

Use the Checklist to analyze Theme in *Roll of Thunder, Hear My Cry*. Refer to the sample student annotations about Theme in the text.

••• CHECKLIST FOR THEME

In order to identify a theme or central idea in a text, note the following:

✓ the topic of the text

✓ whether or not the theme is stated directly in the text

✓ details in the text that may reveal the theme

- the title and chapter headings

- details about the setting

- a narrator's or speaker's tone

- characters' thoughts, actions, and dialogue

- the central conflict in the story's plot

- the resolution of the conflict

- what the characters learn through their experiences

✓ analyze how characters are affected by the setting, the other characters, and the problems they face and what impact these may have on how the theme is developed

To determine a theme or central idea of a text and how it is conveyed through particular details, consider the following questions:

✓ What theme, message, or central idea is being communicated in the text?

✓ What details helped to reveal that theme or central idea?

✓ When did you become aware of that theme? For instance, did the story's conclusion reveal the theme?

Skill:
Theme

Reread paragraphs 1–8 of *Roll of Thunder, Hear My Cry*. Then, using the Checklist on the previous page, answer the multiple-choice questions below.

⟳ YOUR TURN

1. What can the reader infer about Mrs. Logan from these lines of dialogue?

   ○ A. She is shy about speaking to her husband.
   ○ B. She is not afraid to confront problems head on.
   ○ C. She expects her husband to protect her.
   ○ D. She feels easily scared over small events.

2. What can the reader infer about Mr. Logan from these lines of dialogue?

   ○ A. He doesn't trust his wife with information.
   ○ B. He is often silent during a conflict.
   ○ C. He remains reasonable in the face of conflict.
   ○ D. He is quick to anger.

3. What theme can readers infer from the dialogue between Mr. and Mrs. Logan?

   ○ A. It's best for a family if secrets are kept from the children.
   ○ B. When a person feels fear, he or she should back down from a conflict.
   ○ C. Don't go looking for trouble, but don't shy away from defending your rights either.
   ○ D. It's best to ignore problems until they work themselves out or go away on their own.

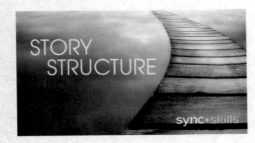

Skill:
Story Structure

Use the Checklist to analyze Story Structure in *Roll of Thunder, Hear My Cry*. Refer to the sample student annotations about Story Structure in the text.

••• CHECKLIST FOR STORY STRUCTURE

In order to identify how a particular sentence, chapter, scene or stanza fits into the overall structure of a text, note the following:

- ✓ the author's use of description, dialogue, and narration and how each develops the events of the plot

- ✓ the pattern the author uses to organize the events within a story or chapter

  - chronological, or in time order

  - events out of time order

- ✓ any literary devices the author uses, such as flashback, a part of a story that shows something that happened in the past

- ✓ any particular sentence, chapter, scene, or a stanza in a poem that contributes to the development of the setting, the plot, and the theme

- ✓ how a particular sentence, chapter, scene, or a stanza in a poem fit into the overall structure

To analyze how a particular sentence, chapter, scene, or stanza fits into the overall structure of a text and contributes to the development of the theme, setting, or plot, consider the following questions:

- ✓ What are the key events in the story and when did they take place?

- ✓ What impact does the order of events that take place in the story have on the theme, setting, or plot?

- ✓ What literary devices does the author use? How does it affect the development of the plot?

- ✓ How does a particular sentence, chapter, scene, or a stanza in a poem fits into the overall structure? How do they contribute to the development of the theme, setting, or plot?

Skill:
Story Structure

Reread paragraphs 22–26 of *Roll of Thunder, Hear My Cry*. Then, using the Checklist on the previous page, answer the multiple-choice questions below.

⟳ YOUR TURN

1. This question has two parts. First, answer Part A. Then, answer Part B.

   Part A: Which of the following statements best summarizes how the dialogue in this passage moves the plot forward?

   ○ A. Farmers are making less money even though they're planting more cotton.

   ○ B. Mr. Avery doesn't need anything from Vicksburg on this trip.

   ○ C. Mr. Avery and Mr. Lanier need to give Mr. Granger 60 percent of their cotton.

   ○ D. Mr. Avery is backing out of shopping in Vicksburg because Mr. Granger is threatening him.

   Part B: Which of the following lines of dialogue BEST supports the summary selected in Part A?

   ○ A. "You goin' to the store tomorrow, David?"

   ○ B. "Your wife brought down that list of things you need yesterday."

   ○ C. "It's—it's that list I come 'bout, David... I don't want them things no more."

   ○ D. "The way cotton sells these days, seems the more we plant, the less money we gets anyways."

Close Read

Reread *Roll of Thunder, Hear My Cry*. As you reread, complete the Skills Focus questions below. Then use your answers and annotations from the questions to help you complete the Write activity.

◎ SKILLS FOCUS

1. Reread the last paragraph of the excerpt. Analyze how the trees in the Logans' backyard symbolize, or represent, their relationship with people like Thurston Wallace.

2. Identify parts of *Roll of Thunder, Hear My Cry* where the author uses specific words and phrases to create a tense atmosphere and how this relates to the overall plot.

3. Locate the word *sloping*. Analyze how the word functions in the sentence to help you determine which dictionary definition best represents the meaning of *sloping* in this context.

4. Identify parts in the story that show how Cassie's relationship with her family impacts her life and helps her see things in a new way.

✎ WRITE

DISCUSSION: In this excerpt, the author builds and releases tension through events in the plot. With each new challenge that the characters have to face, a new theme is revealed or suggested. Overall, do you feel that the author's themes, or messages, are positive or negative? As you prepare for your discussion, use specific parts of the text as well as supporting details to help you form an opinion. Additionally, include any lingering questions you have regarding characters and events.

Teenagers

POETRY
Pat Mora
1991

Introduction

Pat Mora (b. 1942) is a celebrated Mexican-American author whose bilingual works explore themes of culture and identity among families in Texas and along the Southwestern border, where Mora was born and raised. Her 1991 poem "Teenagers" is written from the point of view of a parent who feels they have lost touch with their teenage children. In this brief, fourteen-line poem, Mora reflects upon a universal experience both parents and children endure as they age.

"Doors and lips shut and we become strangers in our own home."

NOTES

1 One day they disappear
2 into their rooms.
3 Doors and lips shut
4 and we become strangers
5 in our own home.

6 I **pace** the hall, hear whispers,
7 a **code** I knew but can't remember,
8 mouthed by mouths I taught to speak.

9 Years later the door opens.
10 I see faces I once held,
11 open as sunflowers in my hands. I see
12 **familiar** skin now stretched on long bodies
13 that move past me
14 glowing almost like pearls.

"Teenagers" by Pat Mora is reprinted with permission from the publisher of "Communion" (© 1991 Arte Público Press - University of Houston)

Skill: Figurative Language

The poet uses a simile. The speaker describes the children's faces "as" sunflowers. A sunflower's petals are not closed up like a rose. I think this means the speaker's children were open to learning from her when they were younger.

First Read

Read "Teenagers." After you read, complete the Think Questions below.

☁ THINK QUESTIONS

1. In lines 4 and 5, the speaker says that "we become strangers in our own home." Who are the strangers in this home? Cite textual evidence to support your answer.

2. Write two or three sentences that explain what happens to the "strangers" when "years later, the door opens"?

3. "Voice" is the way an author uses word choice, tone, and speech patterns to show the personality of a speaker, narrator, or character. Voice gives the sense that a real person is talking to the reader or to other characters. Whose voice is talking in this poem? Cite words and phrases that support your answer.

4. Find the word **code** in the second stanza of "Teenagers." Use context clues in the surrounding stanzas, as well as the stanza in which the word appears, to determine the word's meaning. Write your definition here and identify clues that helped you figure out its meaning.

5. Read the following dictionary entry:

familiar
fa•mil•iar \fə ʻmil yər\ *adjective*

1. closely acquainted
2. sociable
3. having personal knowledge

Which definition most closely matches the meaning of **familiar** as it is used in the last stanza? Explain how you chose the correct meaning.

Skill:
Figurative Language

Use the Checklist to analyze Figurative Language in "Teenagers." Refer to the sample student annotations about Figurative Language in the text.

••• CHECKLIST FOR FIGURATIVE LANGUAGE

To determine the meaning of figures of speech in a text, note the following:

- ✓ words that mean one thing literally and suggest something else
- ✓ similes, such as "strong as an ox"
- ✓ metaphors, such as "her eyes were stars"
- ✓ personification, such as "the daisies danced in the wind"

In order to interpret the meaning of a figure of speech in context, ask the following questions:

- ✓ Does any of the descriptive language in the text compare two seemingly unlike things?
- ✓ Do any descriptions include the words "like" or "as" that indicate a simile?
- ✓ Is there a direct comparison that suggests a metaphor?
- ✓ Is a human quality used to describe an animal, object, force of nature or idea in a way that suggests personification?
- ✓ How does the use of this figure of speech change your understanding of the thing or person being described?

In order to analyze the impact of figurative language on the meaning of a text, use the following questions as a guide:

- ✓ Where does figurative language appear in the text? What does it mean?
- ✓ Why does the author use figurative language rather than literal language?

 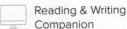

Skill:
Figurative Language

Reread "Teenagers." Then, using the Checklist on the previous page, answer the multiple-choice questions below.

↻ YOUR TURN

1. The poet uses a metaphor comparing whispers to a code for the purpose of —

   ○ A. showing that the speaker cannot hear the voices.
   ○ B. illustrating that the language the teenagers use is not something she understands.
   ○ C. suggesting that the teenagers are writing secret notes.
   ○ D. saying the speaker fears that the teenagers are talking about her.

2. Based on the examples of figurative language in the poem, you can infer that the speaker—

   ○ A. is afraid to admit that her children are grown and are now moving out into the wider world as adults.
   ○ B. still does not understand her children even though they are now familiar again and have grown into strong and tall young adults.
   ○ C. enjoyed holding her children's faces and teaching them when they were younger, but is gratified that they have grown into fine young adults.
   ○ D. is angry that so much time has passed with her teenagers behind closed doors and unwilling to communicate.

Please note that excerpts and passages in the StudySync® library and this workbook are intended as touchstones to generate interest in an author's work. The excerpts and passages do not substitute for the reading of entire texts, and StudySync® strongly recommends that students seek out and purchase the whole literary or informational work in order to experience it as the author intended. Links to online resellers are available in our digital library. In addition, complete works may be ordered through an authorized reseller by filling out and returning to StudySync® the order form enclosed in this workbook.

Reading & Writing Companion   27

Close Read

Reread "Teenagers." As you reread, complete the Skills Focus questions below. Then use your answers and annotations from the questions to help you complete the Write activity.

◎ SKILLS FOCUS

1. Use textual evidence to infer what the speaker means when she writes "a code I knew but can't remember."

2. Identify examples of similes and metaphors in the poem and explain what purpose the poet achieves by using this figurative language.

3. Identify and explain the ways in which the poem explores how relationships impact our lives.

✏ WRITE

LITERARY ANALYSIS: In the poem "Teenagers," a parent talks about her teenage children and how they have changed over time. How does the poem show the speaker's character? Identify examples of figurative language that help the reader understand the speaker. Respond using evidence from the text.

Tableau

POETRY
Countee Cullen
1925

Introduction

"Tableau" was published in 1925 during the peak of the Harlem Renaissance. Its author, Countee Cullen (1903–1946), was one of the leading poetic voices throughout the African American neighborhood's cultural explosion, and would go on to publish multiple books during his lifetime. In "Tableau," Cullen speaks to his unique perspective of walking through both white and black universes, and the joys and challenges that sprang from blacks and whites attempting to forge relationships during this time.

"The golden splendor of the day
The sable pride of night."

NOTES

Skill: Poetic
Elements and
Structure

This Stanza helps me to understand the setting. Two boys are walking together outside. The poet describes the white boy as "golden splendor of the day," while the black boy is the "sable pride of night."

This Stanza helps me understand that some people were not happy to see boys of two different races walking together as friends. I think one theme of the poem is that not everyone celebrates diversity.

1 Locked arm in arm they cross the way
2 The black boy and the white,
3 The golden **splendor** of the day
4 The sable pride of night.

5 From lowered blinds the dark folk stare
6 And here the **fair** folk talk,
7 **Indignant** that these two should dare
8 In **unison** to walk.

9 **Oblivious** to look and word
10 They pass, and see no wonder
11 That lightning brilliant as a sword
12 Should blaze the path of thunder.

Copyrights held by The Amistad Research Center, Tulane University
Administered by Thompson and Thompson, Brooklyn, NY

First Read

Read "Tableau." After you read, complete the Think Questions below.

☁ THINK QUESTIONS

1. How does the poet contrast the two boys in the first stanza? Cite textual evidence from the poem to support your answer.

2. Write two to three sentences explaining what people likely think about the two boys in the second stanza.

3. A metaphor is a figure of speech that compares two seemingly unlike things but implies a comparison instead of stating it directly with the words "like" or "as." In stanza 3, what is the boys' passing compared to? What do you think the metaphor means?

4. Find the word **oblivious** in line 9 of "Tableau." Use context clues in the surrounding lines, as well as the line in which the word appears, to determine the word's meaning. Write your definition here and identify clues that helped you figure out its meaning.

5. Read the following dictionary entry:

unison

u•ni•son \'yü-nə-sən\ noun

1. singing parts of a song together
2. at the same time
3. all elements in one place

Which definition most closely matches the meaning of **unison** as it is used in the second stanza? Write the correct definition of *unison* here. Then explain how you figured out the correct meaning.

Please note that excerpts and passages in the StudySync® library and this workbook are intended as touchstones to generate interest in an author's work. The excerpts and passages do not substitute for the reading of entire texts, and StudySync® strongly recommends that students seek out and purchase the whole literary or informational work in order to experience it as the author intended. Links to online resellers are available in our digital library. In addition, complete works may be ordered through an authorized reseller by filling out and returning to StudySync® the order form enclosed in this workbook.

Reading & Writing Companion   **31**

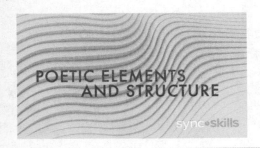

Skill:
Poetic Elements and Structure

Use the Checklist to analyze Poetic Elements and Structure in "Tableau." Refer to the sample student annotations about Poetic Elements and Structure in the text.

••• CHECKLIST FOR POETIC ELEMENTS AND STRUCTURE

In order to identify elements of poetic structure, note the following:

✓ how the words and lines are arranged

✓ the form and overall structure of the poem

✓ the rhyme, rhythm, and meter, if present

✓ how the arrangement of lines and stanzas in the poem contribute to the poem's theme, or message

To analyze how a particular stanza fits into the overall structure of a poem and contributes to the development of the theme, consider the following questions:

✓ What poetic form does the poet use? What is the structure?

✓ How do the lengths of the lines and stanzas affect the meaning?

✓ How does a poem's stanza fit into the structure of the poem overall?

✓ How does the form and structure affect the poem's meaning?

✓ In what way does a specific stanza contribute to the poem's theme?

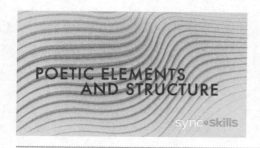

Skill:
Poetic Elements and Structure

Reread lines 9–12 of "Tableau." Then, using the Checklist on the previous page, answer the multiple-choice questions below.

↻ YOUR TURN

1. Lines 9–10 reveal . . .

   ○ A. the boys are impolite as they ignore their neighbors.
   ○ B. the conflict in the poem.
   ○ C. the boys' proud nature as they walk together.
   ○ D. the importance of the setting in the poem.

2. What theme does stanza 3 reveal?

   ○ A. Don't judge a book by its cover.
   ○ B. Be confident when doing the right thing.
   ○ C. Ignoring others leads to the path of justice.
   ○ D. Gossiping is wrong.

Close Read

Reread "Tableau." As you reread, complete the Skills Focus questions below. Then use your answers and annotations from the questions to help you complete the Write activity.

◎ SKILLS FOCUS

1. Identify lines in the poem that help contribute to the poem's overall theme.

2. Identify places in the poem where Cullen uses figurative language, and explain how this language contributes to the poem's meaning.

3. Countee Cullen's poem "Tableau" reads like a story. Identify and explain the events in the poem and how they explore the way relationships impact our lives.

✏ WRITE

LITERARY ANALYSIS: In "Tableau," the poet Countee Cullen describes an unlikely pair of friends. How does the poet use specific stanzas and lines to focus on the theme of friendship? Use evidence from the text to support your response.

The Voice in My Head

INFORMATIONAL TEXT
Holly Warlick
2017

Introduction

In this essay from *The Players' Tribune,* Tennessee Lady Vols women's basketball coach Holly Warlick (b. 1958) speaks to her profound and life-altering relationship with her mentor, legendary coach Pat Summitt (1952–2016). Summitt's eight NCAA titles place her among the winningest college basketball coaches of all time. Yet she is remembered as much for her advocacy for women's sports—and her deep regard for the development of her players outside of the sport—as she is for her impressive championship record.

"She'd break you down . . . and yet you'd show up the next day."

1   I remember the first time Pat Summitt ever watched me play basketball.

2   I was a senior in high school — a small, quick point guard from the Knoxville area — and Pat was the new Tennessee Lady Vols head coach. It was 1975. She was only six years older than me.

3   "You've got to come and see this girl play," someone had told her. There wasn't much recruiting back then — not like there is today. A coach would show up, and if they liked what they saw, that was it.

4   Pat didn't like what she saw.

5   I didn't even finish the game — I sprained my ankle real bad.

6   She left the gym, and I never heard from her again.

7   It's a good thing I was fast. I ran track in high school as well, and won the state championship in the 400 (it was yards back then, not meters). My speed got me the scholarship to Tennessee.

8   But while running came naturally to me, it wasn't what I loved — basketball was. I'd played since I was 10. My dad, Bill, who was a coach, taught me how to dribble. I'd run dribbling drills around chairs, and play with my older brother and our neighbors in the street for as long as it was light outside.

9   Back then, girls weren't allowed to play full-court basketball — just half-court, three-on-three. It was thought that girls' bodies couldn't handle the strain and physicality of full-court basketball. But I knew otherwise. I knew that I could handle it, and that playing with the boys only made me tougher, and made me better. My dad knew it, too. He encouraged it.

10 I tried to walk on to the basketball team my freshman year before my track career even started. I hadn't seen Pat since I had blown it in high school. I'd met some of her players, though, and asked about her — asked what to expect.

11 "She's hard."

12 "She's tough."

13 Every single player said the same thing. Not that I cared — I just wanted to play. And, I figured, at least I was in shape. How bad could it be?

14 I walked into the gym on the first day of tryouts. *Does she remember me?* I thought. *Nope, no recognition.* Pat put us on the line and blew her whistle.

15 Suicides. A lot of suicides. Then she put 30 minutes on the clock for a continuous four-on-two fast break.

16 And that was just the warmup.

17 "That woman is crazy," I said to myself after walking out of the gym that day. "What am I getting myself into?"

18 But I went back the next day, and the day after that. She had that way about her. She'd break you down . . . and yet you'd show up the next day. You wanted to prove to her that you could take it. It took me years to realize that she didn't care about players proving it to her.

19 She cared about players proving it to themselves.

• • •

20 I made the team.

21 "You didn't even recruit her," people would say to Pat years later.

22 "Yeah, I recruited her," Pat would deadpan. "She wasn't very good."

23 She had one drill in practice that she named after me. "This is a Holly day!" she'd yell. Everyone would line up and run suicides, while I had to make 10 layups in a row, sprinting from one end of the court to the other. I was notorious for missing layups because I was too fast — I'd run full speed and my momentum would carry me too far under the basket. I'd make eight in a row and then miss. Every single one of us would have to start over again. It was brutal.

24 She was brutal.

25 But she was building us. She was also building her own legacy, though it probably didn't feel like that at the time. She made $250 a month to coach, recruit, wash our uniforms and drive the team van. (She had a habit of

multitasking behind the wheel generally: speeding, applying mascara and — when cellphones became a thing — talking on the phone.) She was also fighting for equal opportunities for women's basketball — not just our program — at every turn. She demanded the best from people and her players. It was the only way she knew, and it worked. Wins and championships followed.

26 In 1985, a few years after I graduated, I got a call from Pat. In that time, I'd played professionally in the Women's Professional Basketball League for a year, and was working at the University of Nebraska as an assistant coach.

27 "Would you be interested in coming here to coach?" she asked me.

28 "I can be there in 18 hours," I said.

29 The coaching dynamic between us — head coach and assistant — wasn't all that different from the dynamic between us when I was a player and she was my coach. As a player, Pat pushed me harder than others because she knew I could take it. She would give me the hardest defensive assignments, or yell at me a little louder than she would at everybody else. When I became her assistant, she kept challenging me. Our basketball philosophy was the same — how could it not be? But she knew when, how and just how far to push me.

30 She called me Warlick. I called her Summitt.

31 Eventually, through all the time we spent together, especially traveling to road games or going on recruiting trips, that dynamic shifted to something more like friendship. Everyone knows about Pat's icy stare and tough persona, but she was also a loving matriarch with a quick wit. She was someone you always wanted to be around because you never knew what was going to come out of her mouth or happen next.

· · ·

32 I was the buffer between Pat and the players.

33 I'm not sure how it got started, but that's how it worked: She'd chew them out, and I'd remind them that they were O.K. I "survived" Pat myself. Everyone survives.

34 Our players — they were just kids — would come in knowing that she was going to be tough. But they still didn't really *know*. Not until they got here. So, that was my role: to listen and reassure. Over time, I slowly started to lead some practices, handle scouting and sit in on meetings with parents.

35 And when Pat got sick, I slowly started to take the lead on everything.

36   She was suffering from dementia before any of us knew it. We all knew something was wrong, but we just covered for her. It was *Pat Summitt*, you know? No one ever asked. But when she was diagnosed in 2011, we weren't surprised. She told the staff one night, not long before the news broke, on the back porch at her house. We sat quietly for a minute after that before she cut through the silence:

37   "Now, I can drink all I want because I won't remember," she said.

38   That's Pat, for you. One of the worst days of our lives, and there she was, cracking jokes.

39   I remember being in the locker room with Pat later that season. Her illness had been announced publicly, and as a coaching staff, we were just trying to keep our focus on the game. I was going to be acting as head coach that night.

40   "What do you want to see?" I asked Pat. "Do you want to see a press?"

41   "I want to see you not sweat tonight," she said. "I'm gonna be sittin' beside you, and you sweat so much."

42   We laughed our way through it.

43   Together, over time, Pat and I talked about the **transition** of me becoming the head coach quite a bit. But the truth is . . . she was planning on being here forever. I was planning on it, too.

44   I inherited a lot. How do you fill those shoes? Pat Summitt is a basketball icon who not only built a championship program at Tennessee — but she also made it known the world over. She set the standard for other programs. She created opportunities for women when there had been none before, and her monumental **influence** on the game of basketball made little girls all over the world — little girls who may never have seen the Lady Vols play — feel seen and strong.

45   The expectation for the Lady Vols is to win a championship. It's a wonderful burden — to be known and celebrated for greatness, but to be disappointed in anything that falls short of another championship banner. I wouldn't be truthful if I said it's not a challenge. I've had to grow more in the last five years than the 25 plus that came before.

46   Someone was always going to have to follow Pat.

47   Pat Summitt is a mountain. We're all standing in her shadow.

NOTES

48 I visited her often after she stepped down. We'd take rides on her boat or just spend time on the beach. Pat loved the beach. We'd talk, but rarely about basketball. Just . . . life. Her health was **declining** and I was traveling more, so when I couldn't visit, I'd call.

49 "Pat, turn to channel 25 — so-and-so is playing," I'd tell her. Or, I'd ask, "Hey, Pat, what are you up to?"

50 "You know I'm not doing anything," she'd say.

51 She always made me laugh.

52 Our conversations got more difficult as the years passed. She didn't know she was struggling, but I could see it grow. When people who hadn't seen her in a while would visit, I could see the shock on their faces. Pat Summitt was supposed to be invincible.

53 Last June, I'd gotten a call saying she was in bad condition. I went to the hospice where she was staying. Nikki Fargas and Mickie DeMoss were there — both former assistants — and we sat in Pat's room while she lay quietly. I stepped out for a bit while Nikki and Mickie were telling old stories, laughing up a riot.

54 When I came back, there was Pat, sitting up straight while those two were laughing their way through the past. I walked over to the side of her bed and listened. Pat grabbed my shirt and pulled me close to her.

55 "Pat, you know I love you," I said.

56 She'd been hanging on for so many people. Her whole life was about other people.

57 "You gotta let go," I said.

58 That's one of the last things I remember — her gripping my shirt, pulling me close . . . and letting me go.

59 She knew what was coming.

• • •

60 People say grief is like the ocean — that it comes in waves. But waves is too soft of a description. It feels more like lightning. Sometimes, I'll be driving somewhere and suddenly be struck, crying on my way to the grocery. Grief splits you open. I swear you spend your whole life trying to sew yourself back up.

61 I see her statue every day just outside of our facility. Our court is named after her. There's an empty chair on our bench in her memory. I'm confronted by her loss — personally and professionally — in so many visceral ways. On some level, it's comforting. I'm glad she's still around. She's the voice in my head.

62 Pat's presence when she was alive was so big that the void she left was **inevitably** going to be **vast**. As the Lady Vols' head coach, I am trying now to continue her legacy but when I'm not on the sideline — when I go home and sit with everything — I'm just someone who lost their best friend.

63 I carry the weight of that loss, and the weight of the program. But I'll do that every day with gratitude for her life and all that she imparted. And I'll do it with pride for this team and program, which I love with every fiber of my being.

64 I want to make a difference in these kids' lives — because that's what Pat made in mine.

© 2017 by Holly Warlick. Reproduced by permission of *The Players' Tribune*.

✏ WRITE

PERSONAL RESPONSE: Why do you think it's important to have mentors in your life? Write a response to this question that represents your own point of view. Use examples from the essay "The Voice in My Head" to support your response.

We're on the Same Team

ARGUMENTATIVE TEXT
Jacki Jing
2017

Introduction

Jacki Jing was an NCAA Division I volleyball player at Binghamton University, where she was inducted into the school's Athletic Hall of Fame. Here, she draws from personal experiences to respond to a newspaper article that questioned the difficulty of mastering the sport.

"I had to bleed and I had to sweat just as hard as any other elite athlete."

Jacki Jing
562 Maple St.
Dallas, TX 75215

March 21, 2018

SportsNews
854 Commerce St.
New York, NY 10103

Dear Editor,

1   I was pretty excited recently when I saw a SportsNews article titled, "Why Volleyball Is So Popular." As a former NCAA Division I volleyball player, I was excited to see my favorite sport featured on your website. My excitement quickly turned to disbelief as I read your article.

2   In particular, I was insulted when I read the following passage:

> *Athletes go where they find success. Basketball is a difficult sport to master. Unless you're willing to put in the time and effort and have a certain level of athleticism and hand-eye skills, you will not be successful. You will be pushed out of the sport because of what it demands. In volleyball, those barriers are lower.*

3   Basketball is an incredible sport. It requires talent and athletic ability. Yet the exact same is true of volleyball.

4   Just like basketball, it takes years to hone volleyball skills. Volleyball requires long practices in the gym (or in the sand) multiple times a week. Approaching, hitting, serving, passing—these aspects of volleyball may not look hard. However, playing at a high level requires an athlete to master a very specific **technique** for each skill. In this regard, volleyball is no different than basketball. Anyone can pick up a ball and shoot it at the basket. But it takes a lifetime of practice to be as good as the best NBA and WNBA players. The ladies on the

Skill: Summarizing

Jacki Jing, a former college volleyball player, writes a letter to the editor of SportsNews to say that she has a problem with an article she recently read on the website called "Why Volleyball Is So Popular."

According to Jing, mastering volleyball skills and techniques requires years of practice, especially for high level players. Jing insists that volleyball is an intensely difficult sport to learn and play, and I am neither supporting nor opposing her opinion.

NOTES

Olympic volleyball teams might make it look easy. That's because years of practice have **refined** their movements so they appear fluid and graceful.

5   I remember being a gangly, awkward teen. I had to choose between volleyball and basketball. Every person chooses his or her own path for different reasons. I don't think one sport is better or harder than the other. Personally, I chose volleyball because it **required** work. I had to learn how to control my body. I had to learn how to do more than just jump high. I had to learn how to swing hard and sharp. I had to think fast, move quickly, and use strategy. I had to bleed and I had to sweat just as hard as any other **elite** athlete.

6   I am tired of hearing that volleyball is easy. I resent that this article **implies** volleyball players have somehow chosen an "easier" path. More young women are choosing to play volleyball because it is tough. It is competitive. It is fierce and fun. That's it.

7   As for the young women out there who are thinking about volleyball, I can tell you right now it is my life and my passion. I was not able to become an Olympian. Yet at 30 years old I still play as much as I can. And believe me, I still have not mastered it. I am always refining my skills and my knowledge of the game.

8   Volleyball changed my life. When I think about playing in high school and college, it brings back memories that make me tear up. My teammates are my sisters. I am still friends with some of my biggest rivals from college. The relationships you form when working that hard at something stay with you forever.

Women's volleyball: A tough, but fun, sport

9   I still hold close to my heart some of my biggest wins and hardest losses. I've learned what is necessary to perform under pressure. I've learned how to push myself mentally and physically. I've learned how to work with a large group of people. I've learned what it takes to achieve what I want. I have experienced the highest highs of my life on the volleyball court.

10   SportsNews, volleyball is not girly. It is not any less athletic. It is just awesome.

Sincerely,
Jacki Jing

First Read

Read "We're on the Same Team." After you read, complete the Think Questions below.

☁ THINK QUESTIONS

1. What is the author of the letter's main problem with the SportsNews article? Cite evidence from the selection to support your answer.

2. Why did the author choose to play volleyball? Cite textual evidence from the text to explain the author's reasoning.

3. According to the author, why do young women choose to play volleyball? Provide evidence from the text to support your answer.

4. Find the word **refined** in paragraph 4 of "We're on the Same Team." Use context clues in the surrounding sentences, as well as the sentence in which the word appears, to determine the word's meaning. Write your definition here and identify clues that helped you figure out its meaning.

5. Use context clues to determine the meaning of **implies** in paragraph 6. Write your definition here and identify clues that helped you figure out its meaning. Then check the meaning in a dictionary.

SUMMARIZING

sync•skills

Skill: Summarizing

Use the Checklist to analyze Summarizing in "We're on the Same Team." Refer to the sample student annotations about Summarizing in the text.

••• CHECKLIST FOR SUMMARIZING

In order to determine how to write an objective summary of a text, note the following:

- ✓ in a nonfiction text, examine details to identify the main idea, making notations in a notebook or graphic organizer

- ✓ answers to the basic questions *who, what, where, when, why,* and *how*

- ✓ stay objective, and do not add your own personal thoughts, judgments, or opinions to the summary

To provide an objective summary of a text free of personal opinions or judgments, consider the following questions:

- ✓ What are the answers to basic *who, what, where, when, why,* and *how* questions in literature and works of nonfiction?

- ✓ In what order should I put the main ideas and most important details in a work of nonfiction to make my summary logical?

- ✓ Is my summary objective, or have I added my own thoughts, judgments, or personal opinions?

Skill: Summarizing

Reread paragraphs 5–6 of "We're on the Same Team." Then, using the Checklist on the previous page, answer the multiple-choice questions below.

⟳ YOUR TURN

1. What is the best summary of paragraph 5?

   ○ A. Jing states that she chose to play volleyball because she was awkward.
   ○ B. Jing states that she chose to play volleyball because it was challenging.
   ○ C. Jing states that she chose to play volleyball because it involved jumping.
   ○ D. Jing states that she chose to play volleyball because she got to swing hard.

2. What is the best summary of paragraph 6?

   ○ A. Jing believes young women choose to play volleyball because it is fun not because it is easy.
   ○ B. Jing believes that young women play volleyball because it is tough and competitive not because it is easy.
   ○ C. While Jing knows that many people think volleyball is an easy sport, she believes volleyball is tough.
   ○ D. Jing knows that young women find out that volleyball is tough and competitive after thinking it was an easy sport.

WE'RE ON THE
SAME TEAM

Close Read

Reread "We're on the Same Team." As you reread, complete the Skills Focus questions below. Then use your answers and annotations from the questions to help you complete the Write activity.

◎ SKILLS FOCUS

1. Identify textual evidence that supports Jacki Jing's argument in favor of volleyball.

2. Select a paragraph in Jing's argument. Identify the most important details in the paragraph. Then use the details to summarize the main ideas in your own words.

3. Identify evidence in the letter that indicates how sports relationships affected Jing's life. Use details to summarize the impact of these relationships.

✎ WRITE

INFORMATIVE: In the essay "The Voice in My Head" by Holly Warlick and the letter to the editor "We're On the Same Team" by Jacki Jing, both authors write about the ways they have worked hard in athletics and in life. In a blog post of your own, summarize the ways that each author had to work hard, including challenges they faced and what helped them succeed. Then, explain a situation where you had to work hard to achieve a goal. Include any setbacks you had and how you finally managed to succeed. Be sure to provide textual evidence from the two texts and your own personal experiences to convey your ideas.

The Treasure of Lemon Brown

FICTION
Walter Dean Myers
1983

Introduction

Award-winning writer and former National Ambassador for Young People's Literature, Walter Dean Myers (1937–2014) once said, "I write to give hope to those kids who are like the ones I knew—poor, troubled, treated indifferently by society." Myers was raised in Harlem, New York, and grew up loving stories—both the ones his family told him and the ones he read in books. Much of what he writes is based on experiences from his own life. In the short story "The Treasure of Lemon Brown," teenager Greg Ridley meets a homeless man who teaches him a valuable lesson.

"Didn't I tell you every man got a treasure?"

NOTES

1   The dark sky, filled with angry, swirling clouds, reflected Greg Ridley's mood as he sat on the **stoop** of his building. His father's voice came to him again, first reading the letter the principal had sent to the house, then lecturing endlessly about his poor efforts in math.

2   "I had to leave school when I was thirteen," his father had said, "that's a year younger than you are now. If I'd had half the chances you have, I'd . . ."

Skill:
Point of View

The narrator is describing what happens from outside the story because I see a character's name and the pronoun he. *I know how Greg feels, but not what his father feels. So the point of view must be third-person limited.*

3   Greg sat in the small, pale green kitchen listening, knowing the lecture would end with his father saying he couldn't play ball with the Scorpions. He had asked his father the week before, and his father had said it depended on his next report card. It wasn't often the Scorpions took on new players, especially fourteen-year-olds, and this was a chance of a lifetime for Greg. He hadn't been allowed to play high school ball, which he had really wanted to do, but playing for the Community Center team was the next best thing. Report cards were due in a week, and Greg had been hoping for the best. But the principal had ended the suspense early when she sent the letter saying Greg would probably fail math if he didn't spend more time studying.

4   "And you want to play *basketball*?" His father's brows knitted over deep brown eyes. "That must be some kind of a joke. Now you just get into your room and hit those books."

5   That had been two nights before. His father's words, like the distant thunder that now echoed through the streets of Harlem, still rumbled softly in his ears.

6   It was beginning to cool. Gusts of wind made bits of paper dance between the parked cars. There was a flash of nearby lightning, and soon large drops of rain splashed onto his jeans. He stood to go upstairs, thought of the lecture that probably awaited him if he did anything except shut himself in his room with his math book, and started walking down the street instead. Down the block there was an old tenement that had been abandoned for some months. Some of the guys had held an **impromptu** checker tournament there the week before, and Greg had noticed that the door, once boarded over, had been slightly ajar.

7　Pulling his collar up as high as he could, he checked for traffic and made a dash across the street. He reached the house just as another flash of lightning changed the night to day for an instant, then returned the graffiti-scarred building to the grim shadows. He vaulted over the outer stairs and pushed **tentatively** on the door. It was open, and he let himself in.

8　The inside of the building was dark except for the dim light that filtered through the dirty windows from the streetlamps. There was a room a few feet from the door, and from where he stood in the entrance, Greg could see a squarish patch of light on the floor. He entered the room, frowning at the musty smell. It was a large room that might have been someone's parlor at one time. Squinting, Greg could see an old table on its side against one wall, what looked like a pile of rags or a torn mattress in the corner, and a couch, with one side broken, in front of the window.

9　He went to the couch. The side that wasn't broken was comfortable enough, though a little creaky. From the spot he could see the blinking neon sign over the bodega on the corner. He sat awhile, watching the sign blink first green then red, allowing his mind to drift to the Scorpions, then to his father. His father had been a postal worker for all Greg's life, and was proud of it, often telling Greg how hard he had worked to pass the test. Greg had heard the story too many times to be interested now.

10　For a moment Greg thought he heard something that sounded like a scraping against the wall. He listened carefully, but it was gone.

11　Outside the wind had picked up, sending the rain against the window with a force that shook the glass in its frame. A car passed, its tires hissing over the wet street and its red tail lights glowing in the darkness.

12　Greg thought he heard the noise again. His stomach tightened as he held himself still and listened intently. There weren't any more scraping noises, but he was sure he had heard something in the darkness—something breathing!

13　He tried to figure out just where the breathing was coming from; he knew it was in the room with him. Slowly he stood, tensing. As he turned, a flash of lightning lit up the room, frightening him with its sudden brilliance. He saw nothing, just the overturned table, the pile of rags and an old newspaper on the floor. Could he have been imagining the sounds? He continued listening, but heard nothing and thought that it might have just been rats. Still, he thought, as soon as the rain let up he would leave. He went to the window and was about to look when he heard a voice behind him.

14　"Don't try nothin' 'cause I got a razor sharp enough to cut a week into nine days!"

15   Greg, except for an **involuntary** tremor in his knees, stood stock still. The voice was high and brittle, like dry twigs being broken, surely not one he had ever heard before. There was a shuffling sound as the person who had been speaking moved a step closer. Greg turned, holding his breath, his eyes straining to see in the dark room.

16   The upper part of the figure before him was still in darkness. The lower half was in the dim rectangle of light that fell unevenly from the window. There were two feet, in cracked, dirty shoes from which rose legs that were wrapped in rags.

17   "Who are you?" Greg hardly recognized his own voice.

18   "I'm Lemon Brown," came the answer. "Who're you?"

19   "Greg Ridley."

20   "What you doing here?" The figure shuffled forward again, and Greg took a small step backward.

21   "It's raining," Greg said.

22   "I can see that," the figure said.

23   The person who called himself Lemon Brown peered forward, and Greg could see him clearly. He was an old man. His black, heavily wrinkled face was surrounded by a halo of crinkly white hair and whiskers that seemed to separate his head from the layers of dirty coats piled on his smallish frame. His pants were bagged to the knee, where they were met with rags that went down to the old shoes. The rags were held on with strings, and there was a rope around his middle. Greg relaxed. He had seen the man before, picking through the trash on the corner and pulling clothes out of a Salvation Army box. There was no sign of a razor that could "cut a week into nine days."

24   "What are you doing here?" Greg asked.

25   "This is where I'm staying," Lemon Brown said. "What you here for?"

26   "Told you it was raining out," Greg said, leaning against the back of the couch until he felt it give slightly.

27   "Ain't you got no home?"

28   "I got a home," Greg answered.

29   "You ain't one of them bad boys looking for my treasure, is you?"

30 Lemon Brown cocked his head to one side and squinted one eye.

31 "Because I told you I got me a razor."

32 "I'm not looking for your treasure," Greg answered, smiling. "*If you have one.*"

33 "What you mean, if I have one." Lemon Brown said. "Every man got a treasure. You don't know that, you must be a fool!"

34 "Sure," Greg said as he sat on the sofa and put one leg over the back. "What do you have, gold coins?"

35 "Don't worry none about what I got," Lemon Brown said. "You know who I am?"

36 "You told me your name was orange or lemon or something like that."

37 "Lemon Brown," the old man said, pulling back his shoulders as he did so," they used to call me Sweet Lemon Brown."

38 "Sweet Lemon?" Greg asked.

39 "Yessir. Sweet Lemon Brown. They used to say I sung the blues so sweet that if I sang at a funeral, the dead would **commence** to rocking with the beat. Used to travel all over Mississippi and as far as Monroe, Louisiana, and east on over to Macon, Georgia. You mean you ain't never heard of Sweet Lemon Brown?"

40 "Afraid not," Greg said. "What . . . happened to you?"

41 "Hard times, boy. Hard times always after a poor man. One day I got tired, sat down to rest a spell and felt a tap on my shoulder. Hard times caught up with me."

42 "Sorry about that."

43 "What you doing here? How come you don't go in home when the rain come? Rain don't bother you young folks none."

44 "Just didn't." Greg looked away.

45 "I used to have a knotty-headed boy just like you." Lemon Brown had half walked, half shuffled back to the corner and sat down against the wall. "Had them big eyes like you got. I used to call them moon eyes. Look into them moon eyes and see anything you want."

46 "How come you gave up singing the blues?" Greg asked.

47 "Didn't give it up," Lemon Brown said. "You don't give up the blues; they give you up. After a while you do good for yourself, and it ain't nothing but foolishness singing about how hard you got it. Ain't that right?"

48 "I guess so."

49 "What's that noise?" Lemon Brown asked, suddenly sitting upright.

50 Greg listened, and he heard a noise outside. He looked at Lemon Brown and saw the old man pointing toward the window. Greg went to the window and saw three men, neighborhood thugs, on the stoop. One was carrying a length of pipe. Greg looked back toward Lemon Brown, who moved quietly across the room to the window. The old man looked out, then beckoned frantically for Greg to follow him. For a moment Greg couldn't move. Then he found himself following Lemon Brown into the hallway and up the darkened stairs. Greg followed as closely as he could. They reached the top of the stairs, and Greg felt Lemon Brown's hand first lying on his shoulder, then probing down his arm until he took Greg's hand into his own as they crouched in the darkness.

51 "They's bad men," Lemon Brown whispered. His breath was warm against Greg's skin.

52 "Hey! Rag man!" A voice called. "We know you in here. What you got up under them rags? You got any money?"

53 Silence.

54 "We don't want to have to come in and hurt you, old man, but we don't mind if we have to."

55 Lemon Brown squeezed Greg's hand in his own hard, gnarled fist.

56 There was a banging downstairs and a light as the men entered. They banged around noisily, calling for the rag man.

57 "We heard you talking about your treasure." The voice was slurred.

58 "We just want to see it, that's all."

59 "You sure he's here?" One voice seemed to come from the room with the sofa.

60 "Yeah, he stays here every night."

61 "There's another room over there; I'm going to take a look. You got that flashlight?"

62 "Yeah, here, take the pipe too."

63 Greg opened his mouth to quiet the sound of his breath as he sucked it in uneasily. A beam of light hit the wall a few feet opposite him, then went out.

64 "Ain't nobody in that room," a voice said. "You think he gone or something?"

65 "I don't know," came the answer. "All I know is that I heard him talking about some kind of treasure. You know they found that shopping bag lady with that load of money in her bags."

66 "Yeah. You think he's upstairs?"

67 "HEY, OLD MAN, ARE YOU UP THERE?"

68 Silence.

69 "Watch my back. I'm going up."

70 There was a footstep on the stairs, and the beam from the flashlight danced crazily along the peeling wallpaper. Greg held his breath. There was another step and a loud crashing noise as the man banged the pipe against the wooden banister. Greg could feel his temples throb as the man slowly neared them. Greg thought about the pipe, wondering what he would do when the man reached them—what he *could* do.

71 Then Lemon Brown released his hand and moved toward the top of the stairs. Greg looked around and saw stairs going up to the next floor. He tried waving to Lemon Brown, hoping the old man would see him in the dim light and follow him to the next floor. Maybe, Greg thought, the man wouldn't follow them up there. Suddenly, though, Lemon Brown stood at the top of the stairs, both arms raised high above his head.

72 "There he is!" A voice cried from below.

73 "Throw down your money, old man, so I won't have to bash your head in!"

74 Lemon Brown didn't move. Greg felt himself near panic. The steps came closer, and still Lemon Brown didn't move. He was an **eerie** sight, a bundle of rags standing at the top of the stairs, his shadow on the wall looming over him. Maybe, the thought came to Greg, the scene could be even eerier.

Skill:
Point of View

The speaker describes Greg's feelings and actions. He seems scared and doesn't know what to do.

Greg doesn't know what Lemon Brown plans to do, so neither do I. That's what happens with third-person limited point of view. Is Lemon Brown trying to protect Greg? Or scare the men? Not knowing creates suspense in the story.

NOTES

75 Greg wet his lips, put his hands to his mouth and tried to make a sound. Nothing came out. He swallowed hard, wet his lips once more and howled as evenly as he could.

76 "What's that?"

77 As Greg howled, the light moved away from Lemon Brown, but not before Greg saw him hurl his body down the stairs at the men who had come to take his treasure. There was a crashing noise, and then footsteps. A rush of warm air came in as the downstairs door opened, then there was only an ominous silence.

78 Greg stood on the landing. He listened, and after a while there was another sound on the staircase.

79 "Mr. Brown?" he called.

80 "Yeah, it's me," came the answer. "I got their flashlight."

81 Greg exhaled in relief as Lemon Brown made his way slowly back up the stairs.

82 "You OK?"

83 "Few bumps and bruises," Lemon Brown said.

84 "I think I'd better be going," Greg said, his breath returning to normal. "You'd better leave, too, before they come back."

85 "They may hang around for a while," Lemon Brown said, "but they ain't getting their nerve up to come in here again. Not with crazy rag men and howling spooks. Best you stay a while till the coast is clear. I'm heading out west tomorrow, out to east St. Louis."

86 "They were talking about treasures," Greg said. "You really have a treasure?"

87 "What I tell you? Didn't I tell you every man got a treasure?" Lemon Brown said. "You want to see mine?"

88 "If you want to show it to me," Greg shrugged.

89 "Let's look out the window first, see what them scoundrels be doing," Lemon Brown said.

90 They followed the oval beam of the flashlight into one of the rooms and looked out the window. They saw the men who had tried to take the treasure

sitting on the curb near the corner. One of them had his pants leg up, looking at his knee.

91 "You sure you're not hurt?" Greg asked Lemon Brown.

92 "Nothing that ain't been hurt before," Lemon Brown said. "When you get as old as me all you say when something hurts is, 'Howdy, Mr. Pain, sees you back again.' Then when Mr. Pain see he can't worry you none, he go on mess with somebody else."

93 Greg smiled.

94 "Here, you hold this." Lemon Brown gave Greg the flashlight.

95 He sat on the floor near Greg and carefully untied the strings that held the rags on his right leg. When he took the rags away, Greg saw a piece of plastic. The old man carefully took off the plastic and unfolded it. He revealed some yellowed newspaper clippings and a battered harmonica.

96 "There it be," he said, nodding his head. "There it be."

97 Greg looked at the old man, saw the distant look in his eye, then turned to the clippings. They told of Sweet Lemon Brown, a blues singer and harmonica player who was appearing at different theaters in the South. One of the clippings said he had been the hit of the show, although not the headliner. All of the clippings were reviews of shows Lemon Brown had been in more than fifty years ago. Greg looked at the harmonica. It was dented badly on one side, with the reed holes on one end nearly closed.

98 "I used to travel around and make money to feed my wife and Jesse—that's my boy's name. Used to feed them good, too. Then his mama died, and he stayed with his mama's sister. He growed up to be a man, and when the war come he saw fit to go off and fight in it. I didn't have nothing to give him except these things that told him who I was, and what he come from. If you know your pappy did something, you know you can do something too.

99 "Anyway, he went off to war, and I went off still playing and singing. 'Course by then I wasn't as much as I used to be, not without somebody to make it worth the while. You know what I mean?"

100 "Yeah." Greg nodded, not quite really knowing.

101 "I traveled around, and one time I come home, and there was this letter saying Jesse got killed in the war. Broke my heart, it truly did.

Please note that excerpts and passages in the StudySync® library and this workbook are intended as touchstones to generate interest in an author's work. The excerpts and passages do not substitute for the reading of entire texts, and StudySync® strongly recommends that students seek out and purchase the whole literary or informational work in order to experience it as the author intended. Links to online resellers are available in our digital library. In addition, complete works may be ordered through an authorized reseller by filling out and returning to StudySync® the order form enclosed in this workbook.

Reading & Writing Companion   57

NOTES

102 "They sent back what he had with him over there, and what it was is this old mouth fiddle and these clippings. Him carrying it around with him like that told me it meant something to him. That was my treasure, and when I give it to him he treated it just like that, a treasure. Ain't that something?"

103 "Yeah, I guess so," Greg said.

104 "You guess so?" Lemon Brown's voice rose an octave as he started to put his treasure back into the plastic. "Well, you got to guess 'cause you sure don't know nothing. Don't know enough to get home when it's raining."

105 "I *guess* . . . I mean, you're right."

106 "You OK for a youngster," the old man said as he tied the strings around his leg, "better than those scalawags what come here looking for my treasure. That's for sure."

107 "You really think that treasure of yours was worth fighting for?" Greg asked. "Against a pipe?"

108 "What else a man got 'cepting what he can pass on to his son, or his daughter, if she be his oldest?" Lemon Brown said. "For a big-headed boy you sure do ask the foolishest questions."

109 Lemon Brown got up after patting his rags in place and looked out the window again.

110 "Looks like they're gone. You get on out of here and get yourself home. I'll be watching from the window so you'll be all right."

111 Lemon Brown went down the stairs behind Greg. When they reached the front door the old man looked out first, saw the street was clear and told Greg to scoot on home.

112 "You sure you'll be OK?" Greg asked.

113 "Now didn't I tell you I was going to east St. Louis in the morning?"

114 Lemon Brown asked. "Don't that sound OK to you?"

115 "Sure it does," Greg said. "Sure it does. And you take care of that treasure of yours."

116 "That I'll do," Lemon said, the wrinkles around his eyes suggesting a smile. "That I'll do."

117   The night had warmed and the rain had stopped, leaving puddles at the curbs. Greg didn't even want to think how late it was. He thought ahead of what his father would say and wondered if he should tell him about Lemon Brown. He thought about it until he reached his stoop, and decided against it. Lemon Brown would be OK, Greg thought, with his memories and his treasure.

118   Greg pushed the button over the bell marked Ridley, thought of the lecture he knew his father would give him, and smiled.

Reprinted by permission of Miriam Altshuler Literary Agency, on behalf of Walter Dean Myers. Copyright © 1983, by Walter Dean Myers.

First Read

Read "The Treasure of Lemon Brown." After you read, complete the Think Questions below.

☁ THINK QUESTIONS

1. Why does Lemon Brown consider a harmonica and some newspaper clippings his "treasure"? Cite textual evidence from the selection to support your answer.

2. Write two or three sentences describing how Lemon's heart got broken and how this event contributes to his life as an older man.

3. Figurative language is language used for descriptive effect, often to illustrate or imply ideas indirectly. Expressions of figurative language are not literally true, but express some truth beyond the literal level. What does the figurative expression "the dead would commence to rocking with the beat" tell readers about Lemon's talent as a blues musician? Cite textual evidence from the selection to support your answer.

4. Use context clues to determine the meaning of **commence** as it is used in paragraph 39 of "The Treasure of Lemon Brown." Write your definition here and identify clues that helped you figure out its meaning.

5. Read the following dictionary entry:

   eerie
   ee•rie \'ir-ē\ adjective

   1. mysterious
   2. strange
   3. unexpected
   4. causing fright

   Which definition most closely matches the meaning of **eerie** as it is used in paragraph 74? Write the correct definition of *eerie* here and explain how you figured out the correct meaning.

Skill:
Point Of View

Use the Checklist to analyze Point Of View in "The Treasure of Lemon Brown." Refer to the sample student annotations about Point Of View in the text.

••• CHECKLIST FOR POINT OF VIEW

In order to identify how an author develops the point of view of the narrator or speaker in a text, note the following:

✓ the speaker or narrator

✓ what pronouns the narrator or speaker uses to describe characters or events, such as *I, me, he, she,* or *they*

✓ how much the narrator or speaker knows and reveals

✓ what the narrator or speaker says or does that reveals how they feel about other characters and events in the poem or story

To explain how an author develops the point of view of the narrator or speaker in a text, consider the following questions:

✓ Is the narrator or speaker objective and honest? Or do they mislead the reader? How?

✓ What is the narrator's or the speaker's point of view?

- Is the narrator or speaker "all-knowing," or omniscient?
- Is the narrator or speaker limited to revealing the thoughts and feelings of just one character?
- Are there multiple narrators or speakers telling the story?
- Is the narrator a character within the story or telling the story from the "outside"?

✓ How does the narrator or speaker reveal their thoughts about the events or the other characters in the story or poem? How does the narrator's or speaker's experiences and cultural background affect his or her thoughts?

Please note that excerpts and passages in the StudySync® library and this workbook are intended as touchstones to generate interest in an author's work. The excerpts and passages do not substitute for the reading of entire texts, and StudySync® strongly recommends that students seek out and purchase the whole literary or informational work in order to experience it as the author intended. Links to online resellers are available in our digital library. In addition, complete works may be ordered through an authorized reseller by filling out and returning to StudySync® the order form enclosed in this workbook.

Reading & Writing Companion   61

Skill:
Point Of View

Reread paragraphs 71–77 of "The Treasure of Lemon Brown." Then, using the Checklist on the previous page, answer the multiple-choice questions below.

⟳ YOUR TURN

1. Based on the text in paragraphs 74 and 75, what can you infer about how the author develops the point of view of the narrator in the story?

   ○ A. The narrator describes only what Greg and Lemon Brown are doing, not thinking.
   ○ B. The reader knows how Greg and Lemon Brown are feeling because the narrator is Greg.
   ○ C. The author reveals only what Greg is feeling and thinking.
   ○ D. The reader knows why the characters are acting as they do because the narrator is Lemon Brown.

2. How would the story be different if it were told only from Lemon Brown's point of view?

   ○ A. The narrator would only describe what the men were thinking as they called out from below.
   ○ B. One of the men would be using the pronoun *I* to reveal his thoughts.
   ○ C. The narrator would be asking the reader what he or she thought of the scene.
   ○ D. Only Lemon Brown's thoughts would be revealed to the reader.

3. Which paragraph best reveals Greg's thoughts and feelings about the sight of Lemon Brown on the stairs?

   ○ A. 71
   ○ B. 74
   ○ C. 75
   ○ D. 77

Close Read

Reread "The Treasure of Lemon Brown." As you reread, complete the Skills Focus questions below. Then use your answers and annotations from the questions to help you complete the Write activity.

◎ SKILLS FOCUS

1. Identify the setting of "The Treasure of Lemon Brown" and explain how the setting affects the tone at the beginning of the story.

2. Identify key events in the plot and how Greg's response to Lemon Brown changes throughout the story.

3. Identify the advantages and disadvantages of the author's choice of point of view when trying to understand the scene with the three bad men.

4. Identify how Greg's thoughts, words, and actions help the plot unfold throughout the story.

5. Explain how Greg Ridley's brief encounter with Lemon Brown impacts his life and how it may shape his relationship with his father.

✏ WRITE

ARGUMENTATIVE: Three men, one carrying a length of pipe, arrive at the abandoned building to steal Lemon Brown's treasure. Lemon, with Greg's help, scares them off. Does the author reveal enough about Lemon Brown's treasure for the reader to understand its importance? Do you think Lemon Brown's treasure is worth fighting for? Why or why not? Defend your point of view with evidence from the text.

The Circuit: Stories from the Life of a Migrant Child

FICTION
Francisco Jiménez
1997

Introduction

When Francisco Jiménez (b. 1943) was four years old, he and his family immigrated to the United States. At the age of six, he began working on farms, like other members of his family. Now a professor of literature at Santa Clara University in California, Jiménez said, "I came to realize that learning and knowledge were the only stable things in my life. Whatever I learned in school, that knowledge would stay with me no matter how many times we moved." *The Circuit: Stories from the Life of a Migrant Child* is Jiménez's autobiographical novel about migrant farm workers in 1950s California. It describes how migrant workers would go from farm to farm picking fruits and vegetables—also known as traveling the circuit.

"My mouth was dry. My eyes began to water. I could not begin. . . ."

NOTES

from the Chapter: **The Circuit**

1   It was that time of year again. Ito, the strawberry sharecropper[1], did not smile. It was natural. The peak of the strawberry season was over and the last few days the workers, most of them *braceros,* were not picking as many boxes as they had during the months of June and July.

2   As the last days of August disappeared, so did the number of braceros. Sunday, only one—the best picker—came to work. I liked him. Sometimes we talked during our half-hour lunch break. That is how I found out he was from Jalisco, the same state in Mexico my family was from. That Sunday was the last time I saw him.

3   When the sun had tired and sunk behind the mountains, Ito signaled us that it was time to go home. "*Ya esora,*" he yelled in his broken Spanish. Those were the words I waited for twelve hours a day, every day, seven days a week, week after week. And the thought of not hearing them again saddened me.

4   As we drove home Papá did not say a word. With both hands on the wheel, he stared at the dirt road. My older brother, Roberto, was also silent. He leaned his head back and closed his eyes. Once in a while he cleared from his throat the dust that blew in from outside.

5   Yes, it was that time of year. When I opened the front door to the shack, I stopped. Everything we owned was neatly packed in cardboard boxes. Suddenly I felt even more the weight of hours, days, weeks, and months of work. I sat down on a box. The thought of having to move to Fresno and knowing what was in store for me there brought tears to my eyes.

6   That night I could not sleep. I lay in bed thinking about how much I hated this move.

7   A little before five o'clock in the morning, Papá woke everyone up. A few minutes later, the yelling and screaming of my little brothers and sisters, for

1. **sharecropper** a farmer who farms someone else's land, and in exchange, is allowed to live there

whom the move was a great adventure, broke the silence of dawn. Shortly, the barking of the dogs accompanied them.

8   While we packed the breakfast dishes, Papá went outside to start the "*Carcachita.*" That was the name Papá gave his old black Plymouth. He bought it in a used-car lot in Santa Rosa. Papá was very proud of his little jalopy[2]. He had a right to be proud of it. He spent a lot of time looking at other cars before buying this one. When he finally chose the *Carcachita,* he checked it thoroughly before driving it out of the car lot. He examined every inch of the car. He listened to the motor, tilting his head from side to side like a parrot, trying to **detect** any noises that spelled car trouble. After being satisfied with the looks and sounds of the car, Papá then insisted on knowing who the original owner was. He never did find out from the car salesman, but he bought the car anyway. Papá figured the original owner must have been an important man because behind the rear seat of the car he found a blue necktie.

9   Papá parked the car out in front and left the motor running. "*Listo,*" he yelled. Without saying a word, Roberto and I began to carry the boxes out to the car. Roberto carried the two big boxes and I carried the two smaller ones. Papá then threw the mattress on top of the car roof and tied it with ropes to the front and rear bumpers.

10   Everything was packed except Mamá's pot. It was on old large galvanized pot she had picked up at an army surplus store in Santa Maria. The pot had many dents and nicks, and the more dents and nicks it **acquired** the more Mamá liked it. "*Mi olla,*" she used to say proudly.

11   I held the front door open as Mamá carefully carried out her pot by both handles, making sure not to spill the cooked beans. When she got to the car, Papá reached out to help her with it. Roberto opened the rear car door and Papá gently placed it on the floor behind the front seat. All of us then climbed in. Papá sighed, wiped the sweat off his forehead with his sleeve, and said wearily: "*Es todo.*"

12   As we drove away, I felt a lump in my throat. I turned around and looked at our little shack for the last time.

13   At sunset we drove into a labor camp near Fresno. Since Papá did not speak English, Mamá asked the camp **foreman** if he needed any more workers. "We don't need no more," said the foreman, scratching his head. "Check with Sullivan down the road. Can't miss him. He lives in a big white house with a fence around it."

---

2. **jalopy** an old automobile, usually in disrepair

14   When we got there, Mamá walked up to the house. She went through a white gate, past a row of rose bushes, up the stairs to the front door. She rang the doorbell. The porch light went on and a tall husky man came out. They exchanged a few words. After the man went in, Mamá clasped her hands and hurried back to the car. "We have work! Mr. Sullivan said we can stay there the whole season," she said, gasping and pointing to an old garage near the stables.

15   The garage was worn out by the years. It had no windows. The walls, eaten by termites, strained to support the roof full of holes. The dirt floor, populated by earthworms, looked like a gray road map.

16   That night, by the light of a kerosene lamp[3], we unpacked and cleaned our new home. Roberto swept away the loose dirt, leaving the hard ground. Papá plugged the holes in the walls with old newspapers and tin can tops. Mamá fed my little brothers and sisters. Papá and Roberto then brought in the mattress and placed it on the far corner of the garage. "Mamá, you and the little ones sleep on the mattress. Roberto, Panchito, and I will sleep outside under the trees," Papá said.

17   Early next morning Mr. Sullivan showed us where his crop was, and after breakfast, Papá, Roberto, and I headed for the vineyard to pick.

18   Around nine o'clock the temperature had risen to almost one hundred degrees. I was completely soaked in sweat and my mouth felt as if I had been chewing on a handkerchief. I walked over to the end of the row, picked up the jug of water we had brought, and began drinking. "Don't drink too much; you'll get sick," Roberto shouted. No sooner had he said that than I felt sick to my stomach. I dropped to my knees and let the jug roll off my hands. I remained motionless with my eyes glued on the hot sandy ground. All I could hear was the drone of insects. Slowly I began to recover. I poured water over my face and neck and watched the dirty water run down my arms to the ground.

19   I still felt a little dizzy when we took a break to eat lunch. It was past two o'clock and we sat underneath a large walnut tree that was on the side of the road. While we ate, Papá jotted down the number of boxes we had picked. Roberto drew designs on the ground with a stick. Suddenly I noticed Papá's face turn pale as he looked down the road. "Here comes the school bus," he whispered loudly in alarm. Instinctively, Roberto and I ran and hid in the vineyards. We did not want to get in trouble for not going to school. The neatly dressed boys about my age got off. They carried books under their arms. After they crossed the street, the bus drove away. Roberto and I came out from hiding and joined Papá. "*Tienen que tener cuidado,*" he warned us.

3. **kerosene lamp** a handheld lamp that burned liquid fuel for light

20   After lunch we went back to work. The sun kept beating down. The buzzing insects, the wet sweat, and the hot dry dust made the afternoon seem to last forever. Finally the mountains around the valley reached out and swallowed the sun. Within an hour it was too dark to continue picking. The vines blanketed the grapes, making it difficult to see the bunches. "*Vámanos*," said Papá, signaling to us that it was time to quit work. Papá then took out a pencil and began to figure out how much we had earned our first day. He wrote down numbers, crossed some out, wrote down some more, "*Quince*," he murmured.

21   When we arrived home, we took a cold shower underneath a water hose. We then sat down to eat dinner around some wooden crates that served as a table. Mamá had cooked a special meal for us. We had rice and tortillas with *carne con chile,* my favorite dish.

22   The next morning I could hardly move. My body ached all over. I felt little control over my arms and legs. This feeling went on every morning for days until my muscles finally got used to the work.

23   It was Monday, the first week of November. The grape season was over and I could now go to school. I woke up early that morning and lay in bed, looking at the stars and **savoring** the thought of not going to work and of starting sixth grade for the first time that year. Since I could not sleep, I decided to get up and join Papá and Roberto at breakfast. I sat at the table across from Roberto, but I kept my head down. I did not want to look up and face him. I knew he was sad. He was not going to school today. He was not going tomorrow, or next week, or next month. He would not go until the cotton season was over, and that was sometime in February. I rubbed my hands together and watched the dry, acid stained skin fall to the floor in little rolls.

24   When Papá and Roberto left for work, I felt relief. I walked to the top of a small grade next to the shack and watched the *Carcachita* disappear in the distance in a cloud of dust.

25   Two hours later, around eight o'clock, I stood by the side of the road waiting for school bus number twenty. When it arrived I climbed in. Everyone was busy either talking or yelling. I sat in an empty seat in the back.

26   When the bus stopped in front of the school, I felt very nervous. I looked out the bus window and saw boys and girls carrying books under their arms. I put my hands in my pant pockets and walked to the principal's office. When I entered I heard a woman's voice say: "May I help you?" I was startled. I had not heard English for months. For a few seconds I remained speechless. I looked at the lady who waited for an answer. My first instinct was to answer her in Spanish, but I held back. Finally, after struggling for English words, I

NOTES

managed to tell her that I wanted to enroll in the sixth grade. After answering many questions, I was led to the classroom.

27   Mr. Lema, the sixth grade teacher, greeted me and assigned me a desk. He then introduced me to the class. I was so nervous and scared at that moment when everyone's eyes were on me that I wished I were with Papá and Roberto picking cotton. After taking roll, Mr. Lema gave the class the assignment for the first hour. "The first thing we have to do this morning is finish reading the story we began yesterday," he said enthusiastically. He walked up to me, handed me an English book, and asked me to read. "We are on page 125," he said politely. When I heard this, I felt my blood rush to my head; I felt dizzy. "Would you like to read?" he asked **hesitantly**. I opened the book to page 125. My mouth was dry. My eyes began to water. I could not begin. "You can read later," Mr. Lema said understandingly.

28   For the rest of the reading period I kept getting angrier and angrier with myself. I should have read, I thought to myself. During recess I went into the restroom and opened my English book to page 125. I began to read in a low voice, pretending I was in class. There were many words I did not know. I closed the book and headed back to the classroom.

29   Mr. Lema was sitting at his desk correcting papers. When I entered he looked up at me and smiled. I felt better. I walked up to him and asked if he could help me with the new words. "Gladly," he said.

30   The rest of the month I spent my lunch hours working on English with Mr. Lema, my best friend at school.

31   One Friday, during lunch hour, Mr. Lema asked me to take a walk with him to the music room. "Do you like music?" he asked me as we entered the building. "Yes, I like *corridos*[4]," I answered. He then picked up a trumpet, blew on it, and handed it to me. The sound gave me goose bumps. I knew that sound. I had heard it in many *corridos*. "How would you like to learn how to play it?" he asked. He must have read my face because before I could answer, he added: "I'll teach you how to play it during our lunch hours."

---

4. **corridos** a traditional Mexican ballad, usually with lyrics describing an actual historical event

32   That day I could hardly wait to tell Papá and Mamá the great news. As I got off the bus, my little brothers and sisters ran up to meet me. They were yelling and screaming. I thought they were happy to see me, but when I opened the door to our shack, I saw that everything we owned was neatly packed in cardboard boxes.

© 1992 by Francisco Jiménez, THE CIRCUIT: STORIES FROM THE LIFE OF A MIGRANT CHILD. Reproduced by permission of Francisco Jiménez.

✏ WRITE

PERSONAL RESPONSE: In *The Circuit*, Francisco and his family are constantly moving. Each time Francisco's family moves, he feels sad to leave yet another place behind. At school, Francisco finds stability with a teacher, Mr. Lema, who helps him with reading.

Have you ever moved? If so, how did it make you feel? If not, think about something in your life that is stable and consistent. How does it contribute to your happiness? How do your feelings compare or contrast with Francisco's? Use newly-acquired vocabulary and evidence from the text to support your response.

That Day

POETRY
David Kherdian
1978

Introduction

David Kherdian (b. 1931) is an Armenian American writer and poet who is best known for penning an account of his mother's childhood during the Armenian Genocide called *The Road from Home*. In total, he has published more than 75 books in numerous genres, from creative nonfiction to poetry, and has also worked as an editor of numerous literary journals and anthologies. In his poem "That Day," presented here, Kherdian reflects on a special memory of his father.

"Just once
and the day stands out forever
in my memory"

1 Just once
2 my father stopped on the way
3 into the house from work
4 and joined in the softball game
5 we were having in the street,
6 and **attempted** to play in *our*
7 game that *his* country had never
8 known.
9 Just once
10 and the day stands out forever
11 in my memory
12 as a father's living **gesture**
13 to his son,
14 that in playing even the fool
15 or the clown, he would **reveal**
16 that the lines of their lives
17 were sewn from a tougher **fabric**
18 than the son had **previously** known.

✏ WRITE

PERSONAL RESPONSE: Using "That Day" as an inspiration, write about a memory of an experience from which you learned something valuable about a family member or friend. Borrow key language from the poem to describe what you saw and felt, along with details and descriptions of your own.

A Poem for My Librarian, Mrs. Long

POETRY
Nikki Giovanni
2007

Introduction

Nikki Giovanni (b. 1943) calls herself a "Black American, a daughter, a mother, a professor of English." She is also the recipient of 25 honorary degrees, as well as an award-winning poet, writer, and activist who gives voice to issues of social justice and identity. In this poem, she adopts the persona of a "troubled little girl" in need of a book to demonstrate how reading can be a revolutionary act.

"You never know what troubled little girl needs a book. . ."

A Poem for My Librarian, Mrs. Long
(You never know what troubled little girl needs a book)

1 At a time when there was not tv before 3:00 P.M.
2 And on Sunday none until 5:00
3 We sat on the front porches watching
4 The jfg sign go on and off greeting
5 The neighbors, discussing the political
6 **Situation** congratulating the preacher
7 On his sermon
8 There was always the radio which brought us
9 Songs from wlac in nashville and what we would now call
10 Easy listening or smooth jazz but when I listened
11 Late at night with my **portable** (that I was so proud of)
12 Tucked under my pillow
13 I heard nat king cole and matt dennis, june christy and ella
14 Fitzgerald
15 And sometimes sarah vaughan sing
16 Black coffee
17 Which I now drink
18 It was just called music

19 There was a bookstore uptown on gay street
20 Which I visited and inhaled that wonderful odor
21 Of new books
22 Even today I read hardcover as a preference paperback only
23 As a last resort

24 And up the hill on vine street
25 (The main black corridor) sat our carnegie library
26 Mrs. Long always glad to see you
27 The stereoscope always ready to show you faraway
28 Places to dream about

29 Mrs. Long asking what are you looking for today
30 When I wanted Leaves of Grass or Alfred North Whitehead
31 She would go to the big library uptown and I now know
32 Hat in hand to ask to borrow so that I might borrow
33 Probably they said something **humiliating** since southern
34 Whites like to humiliate southern blacks

35 But she **nonetheless** brought the books
36 Back and I held them to my chest
37 Close to my heart
38 And happily skipped back to grandmother's house
39 Where I would sit on the front porch
40 In a gray **glider** and dream of a world
41 Far away

42 I love the world where I was
43 I was safe and warm and grandmother gave me neck kisses
44 When I was on my way to bed

45 But there was a world
46 Somewhere
47 Out there
48 And Mrs. Long opened that **wardrobe**
49 But no lions or witches scared me
50 I went through
51 Knowing there would be
52 Spring

"A Poem for My Librarian, Mrs. Long" from ACOLYTES by NIKKI GIOVANNI
Used by permission of HarperCollins Publishers

First Read

Read "A Poem for My Librarian, Mrs. Long." After you read, complete the Think Questions below.

1. Describe the setting of the poem. Cite textual evidence from the selection to support your answer.

2. Why is Mrs. Long important to the speaker of the poem? Cite textual evidence from the selection to support your answer.

3. Poetic structure describes the organization of words and lines in a poem. Examine Giovanni's line breaks. One line often runs into the next. What ideas about the speaker do you get from the way lines 13 and 14 run together? Cite textual evidence from the selection to support your answer.

4. Use context clues to determine the meaning of **portable** as it is used in line 11 of "A Poem for My Librarian, Mrs. Long."

5. Read the following dictionary entry:

   nonetheless
   none·the·less \ˌnən-thə-ˈles\ adverb

   1. in spite of that
   2. by any means
   3. without care

   Which definition most closely matches the meaning of **nonetheless** as it is used in line 35? Write the correct definition of *nonetheless* here and explain how you figured out the correct meaning.

Skill:
Compare and Contrast

Use the Checklist to analyze Compare and Contrast in "A Poem for My Librarian, Mrs. Long." Refer to the sample student annotations about Compare and Contrast in the text.

••• CHECKLIST FOR COMPARE AND CONTRAST

In order to determine how to compare and contrast texts in different forms or genres, use the following steps:

- ✓ first, choose texts with similar subjects or topics

- ✓ next, identify the qualities or characteristics of each genre

- ✓ after, identify the theme or topic in each work

- ✓ finally, analyze ways in which the texts are similar and different in the way they approach similar themes and topics

  - think about what the characters or narrators do and say

  - think about what happens as a result of the characters or narrators' words and actions

To compare and contrast texts in different forms or genres in terms of their approaches to similar themes and topics, consider the following questions:

- ✓ How does each text approach the theme and topic? How does the form or genre of the text affect this approach?

- ✓ What are the similarities and differences in the subjects or topics of the texts I have chosen?

Skill:
Compare and Contrast

Reread paragraphs 28–30 of *The Circuit,* lines 45–52 of "A Poem for My Librarian, Mrs. Long" and lines 9–18 of "That Day." Then, using the Checklist on the previous page, complete the chart below to compare and contrast the passages.

⟳ YOUR TURN

	Observation Options
A	A librarian's special interest in a girl who loves to read prepares the girl to enter the wider world unafraid.
B	Through the help of an understanding adult all the characters find ways to bridge their world with the wider world.
C	A teacher becomes a friend and helps the main character work on his English.
D	A father's willingness to seem foolish shows his son the strength needed to live in a new and strange home.

The Circuit	A Poem for My Librarian, Mrs. Long	That Day	All

Close Read

Reread "A Poem for My Librarian, Mrs. Long." As you reread, complete the Skills Focus questions below. Then use your answers and annotations from the questions to help you complete the Write activity.

◎ SKILLS FOCUS

1. Identify the theme of "A Poem for My Librarian, Mrs. Long." Use textual evidence to explain the theme.

2. Nikki Giovanni writes from her own point of view as a child. How does this help the reader relate to her? Use textual evidence from the poem to support your answer.

3. In *The Circuit*, Mr. Lema gives up his lunch hour to help Francisco improve his reading. Identify evidence in "A Poem for My Librarian, Mrs. Long" where Mrs. Long steps in to help the young Nikki Giovanni. Use textual evidence to compare and contrast what the two authors want their audience to understand when they read about these actions.

4. The boy in "That Day" is deeply touched when his father joins his softball game. Identify evidence in "A Poem for My Librarian, Mrs Long" that reveals how Nikki Giovanni also appreciated Mrs. Long's efforts. Use textual evidence to compare and contrast the responses of the two young people.

5. The impact of relationships on people's lives is one of the messages in *The Circuit*. Grateful for Mr. Lema's guidance, Francisco considers him his best friend at school. Identify textual evidence in "A Poem for My Librarian, Mrs. Long" that shows Nikki Giovanni is delivering a similar message about the importance of relationships. Use textual evidence to explain how relationships have impacted Giovanni's life.

✏ WRITE

COMPARE AND CONTRAST: What theme do *The Circuit*, "That Day," and "A Poem for My Librarian, Mrs. Long" have in common? Write a response in which you compare and contrast each text's theme. Remember to support your ideas with evidence from all three texts, and use newly-acquired vocabulary as appropriate.

Extended
Writing
Project and
Grammar

EXTENDED
WRITING
PROJECT
ARGUMENTATIVE
WRITING

ARGUMENTATIVE
WRITING
PROCESS
PLAN

Argumentative Writing Process: Plan

| PLAN | DRAFT | REVISE | EDIT AND PUBLISH |

In this unit, you have read and learned about how relationships can shape people's lives. Sometimes, the way a relationship influences our lives goes unnoticed, like Phoebe's dismissive, uncaring behavior toward her mother in *Walk Two Moons*. In other cases, a relationship may leave an impression that lasts from childhood to adulthood, as in Nikki Giovanni's "A Poem for My Librarian, Mrs. Long."

WRITING PROMPT

Can relationships shape your future?

Think about the ways in which relationships shaped the lives of characters and individuals in the texts you have read in this unit. Then reflect on your own life. Think of a person who has influenced you in a positive way. Would your life be different if this person were not in your life? Based on your personal experience and at least one text from the unit, do you think relationships can actually shape people's futures? Why or why not? Support your argument with evidence from at least one text and your personal experience.

- an introduction
- a thesis statement
- coherent body paragraphs
- reasons and relevant evidence, which includes textual evidence
- a conclusion that follows from this argument

Writing to Sources

As you gather ideas and information from the texts in the unit, be sure to:

- include a claim;
- address counterclaims;
- use evidence from multiple sources; and
- avoid overly relying on one source.

Introduction to Argumentative Writing

Argumentative writing is meant to convince readers of the writer's position or point of view on a subject. To best support an opinion in argumentative writing, the writer introduces claims, which are statements that explain why he or she agrees or disagrees with the prompt. In order to make a convincing argument, writers may address opposing points of view, or counterclaims, and explain why these are not true in their opinion. Argumentative writing also relies on reasons and relevant evidence to support the writer's point of view. Without specific examples or evidence, an argument wouldn't be very strong.

A successful argument should have the following characteristics:

- an introduction
- a clear thesis statement summarizing the argument's main idea or central claim
- body paragraphs containing specific claims
- reasons and relevant evidence to support the claims
- a conclusion

As you continue with this Extended Writing Project, you'll receive more instruction and practice at crafting each of the characteristics of argumentative writing in order to develop your opinion about whether or not relationships can truly impact people's futures.

Before you get started on your own argument, read the essay that one student, Ellie, wrote in response to the writing prompt. As you read the Model, highlight and annotate the features of argumentative writing that Ellie included in her argument.

☰ STUDENT MODEL

NOTES

1   Has someone ever helped you achieve a goal? While friends, family members, and mentors cannot prewrite our futures for us, they can help us shape them. In Nikki Giovanni's "A Poem for My Librarian, Mrs. Long," the speaker describes how a librarian named Mrs. Long helped her overcome the limits that a segregated city tried to put on her learning. This relationship changed the speaker's life. While I have not faced such a difficult barrier, I did make a connection to my own experience as I read Giovanni's poem. I thought of Mr. Lin because he helped me discover an interest in acting even though I was shy. Based on Giovanni's poem and my experience, I believe that relationships can help shape your future when people provide you with the support you need to overcome barriers and achieve goals.

2   People can run into challenges or difficulties, and other people can impact their futures by helping them find ways to make progress in spite of them. This is evident in "A Poem for My Librarian, Mrs. Long" because Mrs. Long helped the speaker gain knowledge even though Mrs. Long and the speaker both faced segregation. For example, Mrs. Long gave the speaker the means to explore the world: "Mrs. Long always glad to see you / The stereoscope always ready to show you faraway / Places to dream about." The speaker emphasizes that Mrs. Long always encouraged her to pursue her interests in the library. For example, detail about the stereoscope also shows that Mrs. Long provided the speaker with technology that let her learn about many different parts of the world. These efforts helped the speaker find ways to work around barriers that were meant to limit what she could do and discover.

3   In addition to helping others overcome barriers, people can also impact individuals' futures by helping them achieve their goals. For example, in "A Poem for My Librarian, Mrs. Long," the speaker shares her childhood goal of wanting to read more books. She writes, "I wanted *Leaves of Grass* or Alfred North Whitehead." Mrs. Long helped the speaker achieve her goal by going to "the big library uptown" with her "hat in hand to ask to borrow so that I might borrow." After traveling

NOTES

to the main library, Mrs. Long endured "humiliating" remarks from the white librarians. Yet Mrs. Long did not let this stop her. She "nonetheless brought the books" back to the speaker, who read and loved the books. The speaker remembers that after getting the books "I held them to my chest / Close to my heart." Mrs. Long's determination and assistance helped the speaker to achieve her goal of reading more books and encouraged the speaker to continue reading.

4　Although my goals and circumstances are different from the poem, I have been able to achieve a goal due to support from another person. I am extremely shy and feel nervous when I am in groups of people. My hands get sweaty and my voice shakes. Despite my shyness, I have always dreamed of becoming an actress. When our local community center announced they were putting on a production of *Peter Pan*, I wanted to audition for the role of Wendy. I shared this goal with my drama teacher Mr. Lin and explained that I was nervous. Mr. Lin helped me to overcome this barrier by offering me encouragement. He told me that I did not need to be an expert actor. Instead, I just needed to be the best Wendy I could be. He suggested that we start with small steps and had me read the school announcements at the beginning of class. After a couple of weeks, reading the announcements felt like second nature! Once we addressed this first barrier, Mr. Lin suggested that I perform a scene from *Peter Pan* in front of my drama class. Then, he and my classmates gave me helpful feedback that made my final audition much stronger. When I heard I got the part, I knew Mr. Lin's support helped me to achieve my goal.

5　Mr. Lin's mentorship has taught me that I can overcome personal challenges to pursue my dreams. Likewise, the poem "A Poem for My Librarian, Mrs. Long," shows that relationships can have a positive impact on individuals' futures. The speaker explains that: "Mrs. Long opened that wardrobe / But no lions or witches scared me / I went through / Knowing there would be / Spring." In other words, Mrs. Long helped the speaker to open up doors to other worlds and view the future with confidence and optimism. Based on the speaker's experiences in the poem and my own experiences, I believe that relationships can help us to overcome challenges that might otherwise make achieving goals seem impossible. Perhaps they might even inspire us to dream of new and bigger goals, creating a positive and long-lasting effect on our lives.

✏️ WRITE

Writers often take notes about their ideas before they sit down to write. Think about what you've learned so far about argumentative writing to help you begin prewriting.

- Who has influenced you? In what way?

- Would your life be different without this person? Why or why not?

- Drawing from your own experiences and relationships, do you believe that relationships can actually shape people's futures? Why or why not?

Response Instructions

Use the questions in the bulleted list to write a one-paragraph summary. Your summary should include a personal example of a relationship that has influenced you, if your life would be different without this person, as well as your opinion about whether or not relationships can truly shape someone's future.

Don't worry about including all of the details now; focus only on the most essential and important elements. You will refer to this short summary as you continue through the steps of the writing process.

Skill: Organizing Argumentative Writing

••• CHECKLIST FOR ORGANIZING ARGUMENTATIVE WRITING

As you consider how to organize your writing for your argumentative essay, use the following questions as a guide:

- What is my position on this topic?
- Have I chosen the best organizational structure to present my information?
- Can my claim be supported by logical reasoning and relevant evidence?
- Do I have enough evidence to support my claim?

Follow these steps to plan out the organization of your argumentative essay, including organizing your reasons and evidence clearly:

- Identify your claim.
  > Write a statement that will present your claim in the first paragraph.
- Choose an organizational structure that will present your claim effectively.
- identify reasons and evidence that support your claim.

YOUR TURN

Read the statements below. Then, complete the chart by matching each statement to its correct place in the outline.

	Statement Options
A	People can run into challenges or difficulties, and other people can impact their futures by helping them find ways to make progress in spite of them.
B	While friends, family members, and mentors cannot prewrite our futures for us, they can help us shape them.
C	Mr. Lin's mentorship has taught me that I can overcome personal challenges to pursue my dreams.

Outline	Statement
Position	
Claim	
Reason/Evidence	

WRITE

Use the questions in the checklist section to write an outline for your argument.

Skill:
Thesis Statement

••• CHECKLIST FOR THESIS STATEMENT

Before you begin writing your thesis statement, ask yourself the following questions:

- What is the prompt asking me to write about?
- What is the topic of my argument or essay?
- What claim do I want to make about the topic of this argument or essay? Is my opinion clear to my reader?
- Does my thesis statement introduce the body of my argument or essay?
- Where should I place my thesis statement?

Here are some methods to introduce and develop your claim and topic:

- Think about the topic and central idea of your essay.
  - > The central idea of an argument is stated as a claim, or what will be proven or shown to be true.
  - > Identify as many claims as you intend to prove.

- Write a clear statement about the central idea or claim. Your thesis statement should:
  - > let the reader anticipate the body of your essay.
  - > respond completely to the writing prompt.

- Consider the best placement for your thesis statement.
  - > If your response is short, you may want to get right to the point. Your thesis statement may be presented in the first sentence of the argument or essay.
  - > If your response is longer (as in a formal argument or essay), you can build up to your thesis statement. In this case, you can place your thesis statement at the end of your introductory paragraph.

⟳ YOUR TURN

Read the thesis statement questions and responses below. Then, complete the chart by correctly matching each thesis statement question with the appropriate response.

	Response Options
A	The topic of my argument is that my life would be very different if it weren't for my basketball coach, Mr. Montgomery, because he helped me decide that I want to be a basketball player when I grow up.
B	The prompt is asking whether or not relationships can shape people's futures. The prompt is also asking me to argue if my life would be different if a certain person were not in my life.
C	My argument will have an introduction, three body paragraphs, and a conclusion. Since it's a formal argument, I will put my thesis statement as the last sentence of the introduction.
D	My thesis statement tells the reader that I will list reasons for how Coach Montgomery helped shape my future, so it sets up the rest of the argument very well.
E	My main claim is that I think that relationships can shape people's futures because Coach Montgomery shaped mine. My thesis statement will be something like this: Special people in your life can definitely shape your future, just like Coach Montgomery helped shape mine.

Thesis Statement Question	Response
What is the prompt asking me to write about?	
What is the topic of my argument?	
What is the main claim I want to make in my argument, and how can I turn this into a thesis statement?	
Does my thesis statement set up the rest of the argument?	
Where should I place my thesis statement?	

YOUR TURN

Complete the chart by answering each of the questions about your thesis statement.

Thesis Statement Question	Response
What is the prompt asking me to write about?	
What is the topic of my argument?	
What is the main claim I want to make in my argument, and how can I turn this into a thesis statement?	
Does my thesis statement set up the rest of the argument?	
Where should I place my thesis statement?	

Skill: Reasons and Relevant Evidence

••• CHECKLIST FOR REASONS AND RELEVANT EVIDENCE

As you begin to determine what reasons and relevant evidence will support your claim(s), use the following questions as a guide:

- What is the claim (or claims) that I am making in my argument?

- Are the reasons I have included clear and easy to understand?

- What relevant evidence (specific examples) am I using to support this claim?

Use the following steps as a guide to help you determine how you will support your claim(s) with clear reasons and relevant evidence:

- Identify the claim(s) you will make in your argument.

- Establish clear reasons for making your claim(s).

- Explain the connection between your claim(s) and the evidence/examples selected.

Please note that excerpts and passages in the StudySync® library and this workbook are intended as touchstones to generate interest in an author's work. The excerpts and passages do not substitute for the reading of entire texts, and StudySync® strongly recommends that students seek out and purchase the whole literary or informational work in order to experience it as the author intended. Links to online resellers are available in our digital library. In addition, complete works may be ordered through an authorized reseller by filling out and returning to StudySync® the order form enclosed in this workbook.

Reading & Writing Companion

91

↻ YOUR TURN

Choose the best answer to each question.

1. The following is a section from a previous draft of Ellie's argument. Ellie would like to add an example to support the claim she has presented. Which of these would BEST follow and support her claim sentence?

> In addition to helping others overcome barreirs, people can also impact individual's futures by helping them achieve their goals.

- ○ A. I pretended I was acting the part of a volcano expert in a play.
- ○ B. I conducted a research project for my social studies class.
- ○ C. Mrs. Long worked at a library.
- ○ D. Mrs. Long helped the speaker achieve her goal by going to "the big library uptown" with her "hat in hand to ask to borrow" books so that the speaker could read them.

2. The following is a paragraph from a previous draft of Ellie's argument. Ellie has included an unnecessary example that does not support her claim. Which sentence should be deleted from this paragraph?

> (1) Although my goals and circumstances are different from the poem, I have been able to achieve a goal due to support from another person. (2) I am extremely shy and feel nervous when I am in groups of people. My hands get sweaty and my voice shakes. Despite my shyness, I have always dreamed of becoming an actress. (3) Except when I was really little I wanted to be a princess. (4) When our local community center announced they were putting on a production of Peter Pan, I wanted to audition for the role of Wendy.

- ○ A. Sentence 1
- ○ B. Sentence 2
- ○ C. Sentence 3
- ○ D. Sentence 4

✎ WRITE

Use the three questions in the checklist to revise the first few paragraphs of your argument by adding one or more reasons and/or relevant evidence to support your claim(s) and overall opinion.

Argumentative Writing Process: Draft

| PLAN | DRAFT | REVISE | EDIT AND PUBLISH |

You have already made progress toward writing your argument. Now it is time to draft your argument.

✏ WRITE

Use your Plan and other responses in your Binder to draft your argument. You may also have new ideas as you begin drafting. Feel free to explore those new ideas as you have them. You can also ask yourself these questions:

- Have I clearly stated if I agree or disagree with the prompt's question?
- Have I clearly provided claims about whether or not relationships can truly shape one's future?
- Do I provide enough reasons and relevant evidence to support my claims?
- Does the organization of the argument make sense?

Before you submit your draft, read it over carefully. You want to be sure that you've responded to all aspects of the prompt.

Here is Ellie's argument draft. Notice her thesis statement. As you read, identify how she supported her claim through reasons and relevant evidence. As she continues to revise and edit her argument, she will find and improve weak spots in her writing, as well as correct any language, punctuation, or spelling mistakes.

NOTES

Skill:
Introductions

Ellie decides that although her introduction has a clear claim and thesis statement, it doesn't grab the attention of the reader. Ellie connects her relationship with Mr. Lin to the poem "A Poem for My Librarian, Mrs. Long" by Nikki Giovanni. She decides that this connection would make a perfect "hook" for her introduction.

STUDENT MODEL: FIRST DRAFT

~~While friends, family members, and mentors cannot prewrite our futures for us, they can help us shape them. I thought of Mr. Lin because he helped me discover an interest in acting even though I was shy. Based on Giovanni's poem and my experience, I believe that relationships can help shape your future when people provide you with the support you need to overcome barriers and achieve goals.~~

Has someone ever helped you achieve a goal? While friends, family members, and mentors cannot prewrite our futures for us, they can help us shape them. In Nikki Giovanni's "A Poem for My Librarian, Mrs. Long," the speaker describes how a librarian named Mrs. Long helped her overcome the limits that a segregated city tried to put on her learning. This relationship changed the speaker's life. While I have not faced such a difficult barrier, I did make a connection to my own experience as I read Giovanni's poem. I thought of Mr. Lin because he helped me discover an interest in acting even though I was shy. Based on Giovanni's poem and my experience, I believe that relationships can help shape your future when people provide you with the support you need to overcome barriers and achieve goals.

~~In addition to helping others overcome barreirs, people can also impact individual's futures by helping them achieve their goals. In "A Poem for My Librarian, Mrs. Long," the speaker chats about her childhood goal of wanting to read more books. She writes, "I wanted Leaves of Grass or Alfred North Whitehead." Mrs. Long helped the speaker achieve her goal by going to "the big library uptown" with her "hat in hand to ask to borrow so that I might borrow" because Mrs. Long wanted to borrow a book at the library. Mrs. Long endured "humiliating" remarks from the white librarians. Mrs. Long did not let this stop her.~~

In addition to helping others overcome barriers, people can also impact individuals' futures by helping them achieve their goals. For example, in "A Poem for My Librarian, Mrs. Long," the speaker shares her childhood goal of wanting to read more books. She writes, "I wanted Leaves of Grass or Alfred North Whitehead." Mrs. Long helped the speaker achieve her goal by going to "the big library uptown" with her "hat in hand to ask to borrow so that I might borrow." After traveling to the main library, Mrs. Long endured "humiliating" remarks from the white librarians. Yet Mrs. Long did not let this stop her. She "nonetheless brought the books" back to the speaker, who read and loved the books. The speaker remembers that after getting the books "I held them to my chest / Close to my heart." Mrs. Long's determination and assistance helped the speaker to achieve her goal of reading more books and encouraged the speaker to continue reading.

~~Some people think that you make your own future, so the relationships you have with people don't make much of a difference. I like totally disagree. Relationships help you work hard to acheive your goals. Without Mr. Lin's advice, I stil would have been afraid to try my hardest. Although my goals and circumstances are different from the poem, I've been able to acheive a goal due to support from another person. I am super shy and feel totally spooked when I am in groups of people. My hands get sweaty and my voice shakes. Despite my shiness, I have always dreamed of becoming an actress. Even though Mr. Lin was my theater teacher, his helped me to become a better student in my other classes. It was so crazy because I did my research, but I felt nervous, I wanted a good grad. I really really didn't want to get laughed at. In front of the class, I made mine fears go away by remembering what Mr. Lin taught me. I pertended I was acting the part of a volcano expert in a play. I was like the most excited person ever when I got an A. Thanks to Mr. Lin, I'm a great student in all of my classes. He helped me believe in myself.~~

Although my goals and circumstances are different from the poem, I have been able to achieve a goal due to support from another person. I am extremely shy and feel nervous when I am in groups of people. My hands get sweaty and my voice shakes. Despite my shyness, I have always dreamed of becoming an actress. When our local community center announced they were putting on a production of *Peter Pan*, I wanted to audition for the role of Wendy. I shared this goal with my drama teacher Mr. Lin and explained that I was nervous. Mr. Lin helped me to overcome this barrier by offering me encouragement. He told me that I did not need to be an expert actor. Instead, I just needed to be the best Wendy I could be. He suggested that we start with small steps and had me read the school announcements at the beginning of class. After a couple of weeks, reading the announcements

Skill: Transitions

Ellie adds the transitional phrase "For example" to make the connection between her evidence and claim clearer. Ellie also adds "Yet" to highlight how Mrs. Long chose to help the speaker, in spite of the "humiliating" remarks she received.

Skill: Style

Since this argument is an academic assignment, it requires formal language, not slang or a conversational tone. Ellie changed several instances of informal or conversational language. For instance, she changed "super shy" to "extremely shy," as well as "totally spooked" to "nervous." Eliminating her conversational tone helps her essay to sound formal and professional.

Skill:
Conclusions

Ellie needs to remind her reader of her opinion about the prompt's question: Can relationships actually shape your future? After restating her thesis, Ellie decides to end her conclusion with a memorable closing comment: "Perhaps they might even inspire us to dream of new and bigger goals, creating a positive and long-lasting effect on our lives."

felt like second nature! Once we addressed this first barrier, Mr. Lin suggested that I perform a scene from *Peter Pan* in front of my drama class. Then, he and my classmates gave me helpful feedback that made my final audition much stronger. When I heard I got the part, I knew Mr. Lin's support helped me to achieve my goal.

People can influence your future by helping you realize what you're meant to be. Although some may argue that people's influence on our lives often goes innoticed, I don't think that's true. Because of Mr. Lin's influence in my life, I decid what I want to be when I grow up. I realized I wanted to be an actor when I had to give a speech at a dinner for ours team's soccer coach. I wanted to say something from mine heart, but it was pounding in my chest. I remembered what Mr. Lin taught me about speaking, so I took a deep breath and just started talking about how great Coach Healy was and how much we'd miss hers. It felt like I talked forever about all the things she had done for us and all of the reasons we would miss her. Everybody was inpresed with my speaking skills and told me I would be a great actor one day. Because of my relationship with Mr. Lin, I know I *will* be a great actor one day.

~~Mr. Lin could have had a big acting career instead of being a theater camp teacher. But, I am really glad he was my teacher. Just like Mrs. Long changed Nikki Giovanni's life, I think Mr. Lin was part of my life for a reason. My life would have been very different without him. He showed me how to face my fears and act like my words matter. He taught me how to be a good actor and a brave person. He changed how I felt about myself and the goals I have for mine future. And, it's true that relationships with people can really shape your future. I'll never forget the lessons I learned from my favorite teacher, Mr. Lin.~~

Mr. Lin could have had a big acting career instead of being a theater camp teacher. Likewise, the poem "A Poem for my Librarian, Mrs. Long," shows that relationships can have a positive impact on individuals' futures. The speaker explains that: "Mrs. Long opened that wardrobe / But no lions or witches scared me / I went through / Knowing there would be / Spring." In other words, Mrs. Long helped the speaker to open up doors to other worlds and view the future with confidence and optimism. Based on the speaker's experiences in the poem and my own experiences, I believe that relationships can help us to overcome challenges that might otherwise make achieving goals seem impossible. Perhaps they might even inspire us to dream of new and bigger goals, creating a positive and long-lasting effect on our lives.

Skill:
Introductions

••• CHECKLIST FOR INTRODUCTIONS

Before you write your introduction, ask yourself the following questions:

- What is my claim? How can I introduce my claim(s) so it is clear to readers?

- What is the best way to organize my ideas, concepts, reasons, and evidence in a clear and logical order?

- How will I "hook" my reader's interest? I might:

  > start with an attention-grabbing statement.

  > begin with an intriguing question.

  > use descriptive words to set a scene.

Below are two strategies to help you introduce your topic and claim, and organize reasons and evidence clearly in an introduction:

- Peer Discussion

  > Talk about your topic with a partner, explaining what you already know and your ideas about your topic.

  > Write notes about the ideas you have discussed and any new questions you may have.

  > Review your notes and think about what will be your claim or controlling idea.

  > Briefly state your claim or thesis.

  > Organize your reasons and evidence in an order that is clear to readers, presenting your reasons first, followed by evidence.

  > Write a possible "hook."

- Freewriting

  > Freewrite for 10 minutes about your topic. Don't worry about grammar, punctuation, or having fully formed ideas. The point of freewriting is to discover ideas.

  > Review your notes and think about what will be your claim or controlling idea.

  > Briefly state your claim or thesis.

  > Organize your reasons and evidence in an order that is clear to readers, presenting your reasons first, followed by evidence.

  > Write a possible "hook."

↻ YOUR TURN

Choose the best answer for each question.

1. Below is a section from a previous draft of Ellie's introduction. Keeping in mind the organization of the introduction, which sentence does not belong?

(1) People can run into challenges or difficulties, and other people can impact their futures by helping them find ways to make progress in spite of them. (2) I'm a lot like Nikki Giovanni because the relationship she had with her librarian changed her life. (3) This is evident because Mrs. Long helped the speaker gain knowledge even though Mrs. Long and the speaker both faced segregation. (4) For example, Mrs. Long gave the speaker the means to explore the world: "Mrs. Long always glad to see you / The stereoscope always ready to show you faraway / Places to dream about."

○ A. Sentence 1
○ B. Sentence 2
○ C. Sentence 3
○ D. Sentence 4

2. Which "hook" could Ellie add to improve the introduction of her argumentative essay?

○ A. Relationships are important.
○ B. Mr. Lin was the best teacher.
○ C. Have you ever gotten through a tough time with the help of a mentor?
○ D. Some people don't value relationships as much as I do.

✎ WRITE

Use the questions and notes in the checklist to revise the introduction of your argumentative essay.

Skill:
Transitions

••• CHECKLIST FOR TRANSITIONS

Before you revise your current draft to include transitions, think about:

- the key ideas you discuss in your body paragraphs.
- the organizational structure of your essay.
- the relationships among claim(s) and reasons.

Next, reread your current draft and note areas in your essay where:

- the relationships between your claim(s) and the reasons and evidence are unclear, identifying places where you could add linking words or other transitional devices to make your argument more clear and complete. Look for:
  - > sudden jumps in your ideas.
  - > breaks between paragraphs where the ideas in the next paragraph are not connected to the previous.

Revise your draft to use words, phrases, and clauses to clarify the relationships among claim(s) and reasons, using the following questions as a guide:

- Are there relationships between the claims, reasons, and the evidence in my argument?
- Have I clarified, or made clear, these relationships?
- What linking words (such as conjunctions), phrases, or clauses could I add to my argument to clarify the relationships between the claims, reasons, and evidence I present?

⟳ YOUR TURN

Choose the best answer to each question.

1. The following section is from an earlier draft of Ellie's argument. Ellie has not used the most effective transition (underlined). Which of the following could replace *On the other hand* in the following sentence?

> Mr. Lin's mentorship has taught me that I can overcome personal challenges to pursue my dreams. <u>On the other hand</u>, the poem "A Poem for my Librarian, Mrs. Long," shows that relationships can have a positive impact on individuals' futures.

- ○ A. Likewise
- ○ B. However
- ○ C. Below
- ○ D. Nearby

2. The following section is from an earlier draft of Ellie's argument. Ellie would like to add a transition word or phrase to unify sentences 1 and 2. Which of these is the most effective transition to add between sentences 1 and 2?

> (1) The speaker emphasizes that Mrs. Long always encouraged her to pursue her interests in the library. (2) The detail about the stereoscope also shows that Mrs. Long provided the speaker with technology that let her learn about many different parts of the world.

- ○ A. In contrast,
- ○ B. For example,
- ○ C. Lastly,
- ○ D. But,

Please note that excerpts and passages in the StudySync® library and this workbook are intended as touchstones to generate interest in an author's work. The excerpts and passages do not substitute for the reading of entire texts, and StudySync® strongly recommends that students seek out and purchase the whole literary or informational work in order to experience it as the author intended. Links to online resellers are available in our digital library. In addition, complete works may be ordered through an authorized reseller by filling out and returning to StudySync® the order form enclosed in this workbook.

Reading & Writing Companion   **101**

YOUR TURN

Complete the chart by writing a transitional sentence that connects ideas with or between sentences or paragraphs in your argument.

Transition	Transitional Sentence
Transitions that clarify a relationship between a claim and reasons/evidence	
Transitions that make writing more coherent, or clear	
Transitions that provide cohesion, or a logical flow of ideas	

Skill:
Style

••• CHECKLIST FOR STYLE

First, reread the draft of your argumentative essay and identify the following:

- places where you use slang, contractions, abbreviations, and a conversational tone
- areas where you could use subject-specific or academic language in order to help persuade or inform your readers
- areas where sentence structure lacks variety
- incorrect uses of the conventions of standard English for grammar, spelling, capitalization, and punctuation

Establish and maintain a formal style in your essay, using the following questions as a guide:

- Have I avoided slang in favor of academic language?
- Have I varied my sentence structure and the length of my sentences? Apply these specific questions where appropriate:
  - > Where should I make some sentences longer by using conjunctions to connect independent clauses, dependent clauses, and phrases?
  - > Where should I make some sentences shorter by separating any independent clauses?
- Did I follow the conventions of standard English including:
  - > grammar?
  - > spelling?
  - > capitalization?
  - > punctuation?

⟳ YOUR TURN

Read the words and phrases below. Then, complete the chart by sorting them into those that maintain a formal style and those that do not.

	Word and Phrase Options
A	It was like, the best day ever!?
B	researched
C	It was totally crazy that I felt nervous and stuff, caus oh boy, I was ready!
D	believe
E	resaerchd
F	Mr. lin who was my theater camp teacher was the COOLEST teacher ever, dont ya think?
G	It was unusual that I felt nervous because I was prepared.
H	beleive
I	Mr. Lin, my theater camp teacher, helped me become a great student.
J	It was the best day of my life!

Maintaining a Formal Style	Informal Style/Containing Errors

YOUR TURN

Edit the sentences to fix the style mistakes.

Sentence	Corrected Sentence
The assignment was turned in totally too late for my teacher to be impresed?	
even though I erned a poor grad in science I stil wantted to be a doctor.	
He put him notes undernaeth the book.	
It was the craziest thing ever when mrs. Long unnounced the field trip.	
Marissa ate she lunch with me class on Wednesday.	

Please note that excerpts and passages in the StudySync® library and this workbook are intended as touchstones to generate interest in an author's work. The excerpts and passages do not substitute for the reading of entire texts, and StudySync® strongly recommends that students seek out and purchase the whole literary or informational work in order to experience it as the author intended. Links to online resellers are available in our digital library. In addition, complete works may be ordered through an authorized reseller by filling out and returning to StudySync® the order form enclosed in this workbook.

Reading & Writing Companion

105

Skill:
Conclusions

••• CHECKLIST FOR CONCLUSIONS

Before you write your conclusion, ask yourself the following questions:

- How can I restate the thesis or main idea in my concluding section or statement? What impression can I make on my reader?

- How can I write my conclusion so that it follows logically from my argument?

- Should I include a call to action?

- How can I conclude with a memorable comment?

Below are two strategies to help you provide a concluding statement or section that follows from the argument presented:

- Peer Discussion

  > After you have written your introduction and body paragraphs, talk with a partner and tell them what you want readers to remember, writing notes about your discussion.

  > Review your notes and think about what you wish to express in your conclusion.

  > Do not simply restate your claim or thesis statement. Rephrase your main idea to show the depth of your knowledge, the importance of your idea, and encourage readers to adopt your view.

  > Write your conclusion.

- Freewriting

  > Freewrite for 10 minutes about what you might include in your conclusion. Don't worry about grammar, punctuation, or having fully formed ideas. The point of freewriting is to discover ideas.

  > Review your notes and think about what you wish to express in your conclusion.

  > Do not simply restate your claim or thesis statement. Rephrase your main idea to show the depth of your knowledge, the importance of your idea, and encourage readers to adopt your view.

  > Write your conclusion.

YOUR TURN

Choose the best answer to each question.

1. Ellie knows that her conclusion will be stronger if she can summarize how her personal experiences support the claim that other people can help us achieve our goals. Which of the following statements can be added to strengthen her conclusion?

> Mr. Lin could have had a big acting career instead of being a theater camp teacher. Likewise, the poem "A Poem for my Librarian, Mrs. Long," shows that relationships can have a positive impact on individuals' futures. The speaker explains that: "Mrs. Long opened that wardrobe / But no lions or witches scared me / I went through / Knowing there would be / Spring." In other words, Mrs. Long helped the speaker to open up doors to other worlds and view the future with confidence and optimism.

- ○ A. He was the best ever.
- ○ B. Mr. Lin's mentorship has taught me that I can overcome personal challenges to pursue my dreams.
- ○ C. I'll never forget my favorite teacher Mr. Lin and his fun acting classes.
- ○ D. Hopefully, one day you will have a teacher like Mr. Lin!

2. Ellie wants to improve the conclusion of her argumentative draft. One of these sentences can be removed to make her conclusion more logically follow her argument. Which sentence can be removed?

> (1) Mr. Lin could have had a big acting career instead of being a theater camp teacher. (2) Mr. Lin's mentorship has taught me that I can overcome personal challenges to pursue my dreams. (3) Likewise, the poem "A Poem for my Librarian, Mrs. Long," shows that relationships can have a positive impact on individuals' futures. The speaker explains that: "Mrs. Long opened that wardrobe / But no lions or witches scared me / I went through / Knowing there would be / Spring." (4) In other words, Mrs. Long helped the speaker to open up doors to other worlds and view the future with confidence and optimism.

- ○ A. Sentence 1
- ○ B. Sentence 2
- ○ C. Sentence 3
- ○ D. Sentence 4

 WRITE

Use the questions in the checklist to revise the conclusion of your argumentative essay.

Argumentative Writing
Process: Revise

PLAN	DRAFT	REVISE	EDIT AND PUBLISH

You have written a draft of your argument. You have also received input from your peers about how to improve it. Now you are going to revise your draft.

⬅ REVISION GUIDE

Examine your draft to find areas for revision. Keep in mind your purpose and audience as you revise for clarity, development, organization, and style. Use the guide below to help you review:

Review	Revise	Example
Clarity		
Highlight the first few sentences in a paragraph, ensuring that the topic or claim is clearly stated first.	Identify the title, author, speaker or narrator, and names of characters.	This is evident in "A Poem for My Librarian, Mrs. Long" because Mrs. Long helped the speaker gain knowledge even though Mrs. Long and the speaker both faced segregation.
Development		
Identify places where you identify claims. Note reasons, relevant evidence, or specific examples you could incorporate to add support.	Add reasons, relevant evidence, or examples to support your ideas.	But Mrs. Long did not let this stop her. She "nonetheless brought the books" back to the speaker, who read and loved the books. The speaker remembers that after getting the books "I held them to my chest / Close to my heart."

Review	Revise	Example
Organization		
Examine the first sentence in each paragraph. Annotate any paragraph that does not transition smoothly from the previous paragraph.	Add a transitional phrase or sentence to provide coherence among body paragraphs.	When I heard I got the part, I knew Mr. Lin's support helped me to achieve my goal.
Style: Word Choice		
Identify informal words and phrases that do not help convey your purpose or opinion in an effective manner.	Select sentences to rewrite using more formal language.	Mrs. Long's determination and assistance helped the speaker to achieve her goal of reading ~~tons of~~ more books and encouraged the speaker to ~~keep at it~~ continue reading.
Style: Sentence Variety		
Annotate paragraphs, sentences, and words that are unusually long.	Separate long sentences into two sentences or shorten sentences by deleting information that is repetitive or unnecessary.	Mrs. Long helped the speaker achieve her goal by going to "the big library uptown" with her "hat in hand to ask to borrow so that I might borrow." ~~because Mrs. Long wanted to borrow a book at the library.~~ After traveling to the main library, Mrs. Long endured "humiliating" remarks from the white librarians.

✏ WRITE

Use the guide above, as well as your peer reviews, to help you evaluate your argument to determine areas that should be revised.

Grammar: Basic Spelling Rules I

Suffixes and the Silent *e*

Spelling Conventions	Base Words	Correct	Incorrect
When adding a suffix that begins with a consonant to a word that ends with a silent **e**, keep the **e**.	place hope	placement hopeful	placment hopful
When adding a suffix that begins with a vowel or **y** to a word that ends with a silent **e**, usually drop the **e**.	race pore	racism porous	raceism poreous
When adding **-ly** to a word that ends with an **l** plus a silent **e**, drop the **le**.	probable humble	probably humbly	probablely humblely

Suffixes and the Final *y*

Spelling Conventions	Base Words	Correct	Incorrect
When a word ends in a consonant + **y**, change the **y** to **i** before adding a suffix. However, if the suffix begins with **i**, do not change the **y** to **i**.	bounty duty fry	bountiful dutiful frying	bountyful dutyful friing
When a word ends in a vowel + **y**, keep the **y**.	essay joy	essayist joyous	essaist joious

Spelling *ie* and *ei*

Spelling Conventions	Correct	Incorrect
Usually, when **i** and **e** appear together in one syllable, the **i** comes before the **e**.	yield friend	yeild freind
When **i** and **e** appear after a **c**, the **e** usually comes before the **i**.	receive conceit	recieve conciet
However, there are exceptions to these patterns.	seizure weird weigh	siezure wierd wiegh

⟳ YOUR TURN

1. How should the spelling error in this sentence be corrected?

> *Dragonwings* is about the expereinces of a young boy from China who goes to America to join his father, a maker of kites that are beautiful enough to be heirlooms.

- ○ A. Change **expereinces** to **experiences**.
- ○ B. Change **beautiful** to **beautyful**.
- ○ C. Change **heirlooms** to **hierlooms**.
- ○ D. No change needs to be made to this sentence.

2. How should the spelling error in this sentence be corrected?

> A person's heart was weighed right after death to determine whether the person had been guilty of deceit or other sins—that was the beleif of the ancient Egyptians.

- ○ A. Change **weighed** to **wieghed**.
- ○ B. Change **deceit** to **deciet**.
- ○ C. Change **beleif** to **belief**.
- ○ D. No change needs to be made to this sentence.

3. How should the spelling error in this sentence be corrected?

> Because of their stark portraial of the thin, pitiful faces of the poor, Dorothea Lange's photographs changed the way the public perceived the Depression.

- ○ A. Change **portraial** to **portrayal**.
- ○ B. Change **pitiful** to **pityful**.
- ○ C. Change **perceived** to **percieved**.
- ○ D. No change needs to be made to this sentence.

4. How should the spelling error in this sentence be corrected?

> When Rosa Parks courageously refused to give up her bus seat, she committed an incredibly dangerous act, but her bravry helped launch the civil rights movement.

- ○ A. Change **courageously** to **couragously**.
- ○ B. Change **incredibly** to **incredibley**.
- ○ C. Change **bravry** to **bravery**.
- ○ D. No change needs to be made to this sentence.

Grammar: Possessive Pronouns

Possessive pronouns are a kind of personal pronoun. A possessive pronoun takes the place of a person or thing that owns or possesses something. It can come before the noun that is possessed, or it can stand alone in a sentence.

USED BEFORE NOUNS	USED ALONE
Singular: my, your, her, his, its	Singular: mine, yours, hers, his, its
Plural: our, your, their	Plural: ours, yours, theirs
Ever since I can remember, I had wanted to know about the Land of the Golden Mountain, but **my** mother had never wanted to talk about it. Dragonwings	Athene claimed that she had the better right, for the beauty of wisdom such as **hers** surpassed all else. Black Ships Before Troy: The Story of the Iliad

When using a personal pronoun to show possession, make sure the pronoun is in the possessive case.

Correct	Incorrect
The computer quickly stores information in **its** huge memory.	The computer quickly stores information in **it** huge memory.
Our dog is a Labrador retriever.	**We** dog is a Labrador retriever.
The clever idea was **theirs**.	The clever idea was **their**.

⟳ YOUR TURN

1. How should this sentence be changed?

> The red house on the corner is our.

- ○ A. Change **our** to **ours**.
- ○ B. Change **our** to **they**.
- ○ C. Change **our** to **their**.
- ○ D. No change needs to be made to this sentence.

2. How should this sentence be changed?

> She hand shot up when the teacher asked for volunteers.

- ○ A. Change **she** to **him**.
- ○ B. Change **she** to **her**.
- ○ C. Change **she** to **hers**.
- ○ D. No change needs to be made to this sentence.

3. How should this sentence be changed?

> Yours is the third seat in the first row.

- ○ A. Change **your** to **you**.
- ○ B. Change **yours** to **they**.
- ○ C. Change **yours** to **their**.
- ○ D. No change needs to be made to this sentence.

4. How should this sentence be changed?

> Will strummed him guitar and invited everyone to sing.

- ○ A. Change **him** to **he**.
- ○ B. Change **him** to **his**.
- ○ C. Change **him** to **we**.
- ○ D. No change needs to be made to this sentence.

Grammar: Formal and Informal Language

Different types of language are appropriate for different situations. Follow these rules when using formal and informal language:

Rules	Informal	Formal
Using a contraction makes language sound more informal.	I can't do it.	I cannot do it.
When writing an academic essay, it is necessary to use formal language.	We should totally focus on how crazy fast animals are disappearing.	The most important fact to consider about endangered animal species is the rate of their disappearance.
When conversing with a friend, it is appropriate to use informal language.	What's up, Sam?	Hello, Sam. How are you doing today?

The type of language you use affects the tone of your writing or speaking.

Formal	Informal
Papa took the towel Mama handed him, but did not reply immediately. I was just inside the kitchen dipping out the butter beans. I moved closer to the window so that I could hear his answer. Roll of Thunder, Hear My Cry	You ain't one of them bad boys looking for my treasure, is you? The Treasure of Lemon Brown
I resent that this article implies volleyball players have somehow chosen an "easier" path. We're on the Same Team	She was as crotchety and sullen as a three-legged mule, and I was not quite sure why. Walk Two Moons

⟳ YOUR TURN

1. How could this sentence be changed from informal to formal language?

   > Hey dude, what's happenin' today?

   ○ A. Hey, what's gonna happen today?
   ○ B. Hello, what's going on today?
   ○ C. Hello. What are you doing today?
   ○ D. Dude, what's going on today?

2. How could these sentences be changed from formal to informal language?

   > Good afternoon. Please include an example in your essay.

   ○ A. Hey dude, also do an example when you write that essay.
   ○ B. Please include an example in your essay.
   ○ C. Include an example in your essay.
   ○ D. Hello. Make sure to include an example.

3. How can this sentence be changed to eliminate contractions?

   > I'm thinking there's a good chance you won't be able to try the cake today.

   ○ A. I am thinking there is a good chance you won't be able to try the cake today.
   ○ B. I think there is a good chance you will not be able to try the cake today.
   ○ C. I'm thinking there is a good chance you will not be able to try the cake today.
   ○ D. I'm thinking there's a good chance you will not be able to try the cake today.

Argumentative Writing Process: Edit and Publish

| PLAN | DRAFT | REVISE | EDIT AND PUBLISH |

You have revised your argument based on your peer feedback and your own examination.

Now it is time to edit your argumentative essay. When you revised, you focused on the content of your argument. You looked at your use of reasons, evidence, specific examples, and transitions. When you edit, you focus on the mechanics of your essay, paying close attention to things like grammar, spelling, and punctuation.

Use the checklist below to guide you as you edit:

☐ Have I followed basic spelling rules for words with *ie/ei*, unstressed vowels, suffixes, and prefixes?

☐ Have I correctly used possessive pronouns?

☐ Have I used formal language and eliminated informal language?

☐ Have I spelled everything correctly?

☐ Do I have any sentence fragments or run-on sentences?

Notice some edits Ellie has made:

- Used basic spelling rules to correct spelling errors.

- Fixed errors with possessive pronouns.

- Corrected informal language, changing it to have a more formal and appropriate tone.

In addition to helping others overcome ~~barreirs~~ barriers, people can also impact ~~individual's~~ individuals' futures by helping them achieve their goals. For example, in "A Poem for My Librarian, Mrs. Long," the speaker ~~chats about~~ shares her childhood goal of wanting to read more books.

✏ WRITE

Use the questions on the previous page, as well as your peer reviews, to help you evaluate your argumentative essay to determine areas that need editing. Then edit your argument to correct those errors.

Once you have made all your corrections, you are ready to publish your work. You can distribute your writing to family and friends, hang it on a bulletin board, or post it on your blog. If you publish online, share the link with your family, friends, and classmates.

The Other Side

FICTION

Introduction

Many of us know what it's like to wish for superpowers. We might sometimes wish we could do things nobody else can do, or know things nobody else could know. But if we did have these powers, would anyone else understand? For the narrator of the short story "The Other Side," an extraordinary experience leads to complicated feelings and big questions.

VOCABULARY

glanced

looked quickly

instant

a moment; a very short span of time

frowned

turned corners of the mouth down to show displeasure

reached

moved arm to touch or hold

creak

make a sound when moved or stepped on

grasped

held tightly

motionless

not moving

READ

 NOTES

1   I **glanced** at my sister, Alexandria, swaying under the tree in our backyard. How could I explain it? I couldn't keep it a secret. She knew there was more.

2   "What aren't you telling me?" she **frowned**. "This doesn't just happen. What did you do?"

3   In most ways, last Wednesday was normal. The sun took its place in the sky, and like countless times before, our neighborhood slowly came alive.

4 What was unusual was that I woke up early. I can't remember the last time I was up before sunrise. That Wednesday something had woken me. I knew that there was no going back because I would be different.

5 I didn't mention that when I told Alexandria before. Now her eyes were asking me to help her understand.

6 "Listen," I pleaded. "I'm trying to explain."

7 That morning, I slipped out of my bedroom and walked slowly down the hallway. The house was silent and my mom and sister slept peacefully. Our dog, Bella, was curled up somewhere.

8 There was darkness in the hallway but I knew where I had to go. I waited for the floorboards to **creak** but they didn't.

9 I arrived at the front door, standing there **motionless**. At first, I felt the presence on the other side. Something was calling to me and waiting for me. I don't know how long the presence had been there, but it wasn't going anywhere. I didn't try to understand. How could I?

10 I couldn't breathe. I looked at the doorknob for a long, long time. I knew that once I opened the door, I wouldn't be the same. I thought of my family and wondered if they would understand. I wished I'd just stayed in bed.

11 I tried to collect myself, but my heart was racing. I turned the knob and stepped forward.

12 In an **instant** I was aware of *everything*: The colors, the wind, and the earth below me — I understood it and could feel it more than ever.

13 I **reached** out to touch it and I changed forever.

14 I looked at Alexandria, as she **grasped** the tree trunk, her mouth open in amazement. I couldn't imagine how this sounded. I felt guilty for burdening her. At the same time, I felt relieved.

15 "Does anyone else know?" Alexandria asked frantically, not even trying to hide her concern.

16 I shook my head. Who could understand — let alone believe — what I could do now?

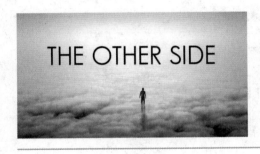

First Read

Read the story. After you read, answer the Think Questions below.

☁ THINK QUESTIONS

1. Who is the story about? How are they related?

    The story is about _____.

    They are _____.

2. Where does the story take place?

    The story takes place _____.

3. How does Alexandria feel at the end of the story?

    Alexandria feels _____.

4. Use context to confirm the meaning of the word *motionless* as it is used in "The Other Side." Write your definition of *motionless* here.

    Motionless means _____.

    A context clue is _____.

5. What is another way to say that the boy *glanced* at Alexandria?

    The boy _____.

Please note that excerpts and passages in the StudySync® library and this workbook are intended as touchstones to generate interest in an author's work. The excerpts and passages do not substitute for the reading of entire texts, and StudySync® strongly recommends that students seek out and purchase the whole literary or informational work in order to experience it as the author intended. Links to online resellers are available in our digital library. In addition, complete works may be ordered through an authorized reseller by filling out and returning to StudySync® the order form enclosed in this workbook.

Reading & Writing Companion   121

Skill:
Analyzing Expressions

★ DEFINE

When you read, you may find English expressions that you do not know. An **expression** is a group of words that communicates an idea. Three types of expressions are **idioms**, **sayings,** and **figurative language**. They can be difficult to understand because the meanings of the words are different from their **literal**, or usual, meanings.

An **idiom** is an expression that is commonly known among a group of people. For example, "It's raining cats and dogs" means it is raining heavily. **Sayings** are short expressions that contain advice or wisdom. For instance: "Don't count your chickens before they hatch" means do not plan on something good happening before it happens. **Figurative** language is when you describe something by comparing it with something else, either directly (using the words like or as) or indirectly. For example, "I'm hungry as a horse" means I'm very hungry. None of the expressions are about actual animals.

••• CHECKLIST FOR ANALYZING EXPRESSIONS

To determine the meaning of an expression, remember the following:

✓ If you find a confusing group of words, it may be an expression. The meaning of words in expressions may not be their literal meaning.

- Ask yourself: Is this confusing because the words are new? Or because the words do not make sense together?

✓ Determining the overall meaning may require that you use one or more of the following:

- context clues

- a dictionary or other resource

- teacher or peer support

✓ Highlight important information before and after the expression to look for clues.

YOUR TURN

Read the following excerpt from the "The Other Side." Then complete the multiple-choice questions below.

---

from **"The Other Side"**

I couldn't breathe. I looked at the doorknob for a long, long time. I knew that once I opened the door, I wouldn't be the same. I thought of my family and wondered if they would understand. I wished I'd just stayed in bed.

I tried to collect myself, but my heart was racing. I turned the knob and stepped forward.

In an instant I was aware of *everything*: The colors, the wind, and the earth below me — I understood it and could feel it more than ever.

I reached out to touch it and I changed forever.

---

1. What does the narrator mean when he says "my heart was racing"?

    ○ A. He is in a competition.

    ○ B. He is in love.

    ○ C. He is nervous.

    ○ D. He is excited.

2. Which context clue helped you determine the meaning of the expression?

    ○ A. "I couldn't breathe. I looked at the doorknob for a long, long time."

    ○ B. "I thought of my family and wondered if they would understand."

    ○ C. "I turned the knob and stepped forward."

    ○ D. "I reached out to touch it and I changed forever."

Please note that excerpts and passages in the StudySync® library and this workbook are intended as touchstones to generate interest in an author's work. The excerpts and passages do not substitute for the reading of entire texts, and StudySync® strongly recommends that students seek out and purchase the whole literary or informational work in order to experience it as the author intended. Links to online resellers are available in our digital library. In addition, complete works may be ordered through an authorized reseller by filling out and returning to StudySync® the order form enclosed in this workbook.

Reading & Writing Companion   **123**

Skill:
Sharing Information

★ DEFINE

Sharing information involves asking for and giving information. The process of sharing information with other students can help all students learn more and better understand a text or a topic. You can share information when you participate in **brief** discussions or **extended** speaking assignments.

••• CHECKLIST FOR SHARING INFORMATION

When you have to speak for an extended period of time, as in a discussion, you ask for and share information. To ask for and share information, you may use the following sentence frames:

✓ To ask for information:

- What do you think about _____?
- Do you agree that _____?
- What is your understanding of _____?

✓ To give information:

- I think _____.
- I agree because _____.
- My understanding is _____.

⟳ YOUR TURN

Watch the "The Lightning Thief" StudySyncTV episode ▶. After watching, sort the following statements from the episode into the appropriate columns:

Statements	
A	Makes me feel bad for him.
B	But Percy is not normal.
C	Do you think he is lying?
D	How do you know Percy is lonely?
E	I can feel it.
F	Can you prove it?

Asking for Information	Giving Information

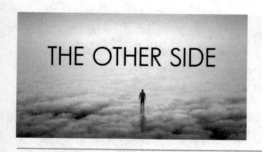

Close Read

NARRATIVE: Think about the end of the story. How has the main character changed? What do you think happens next? Recount the events at the end of the story and describe what you think would happen if the story continued. Pay attention to the *IE* and *EI* spelling rule as you write.

Use the checklist below to guide you as you write.

☐ How was the boy changed?

☐ How does Alexandria feel and what does she do?

☐ How does it end?

Use the sentence frames to organize and write your narrative.

I shook my head. Who could understand — let alone believe — what I could do now?

I couldn't believe that now I _____.

Alexandria was _____.

Then, _____.

Suddenly, _____.

I decided _____.

A Role to Play

FICTION

Introduction

On a day like any other day in science class, Bryan gets unwelcome news. He is assigned a role for a group project. He doubts his own abilities as he thinks back to a role he was assigned for a group project in sixth grade. He had wanted to do well, but he let his group down. Now Bryan must confront his fears and fulfill his role. Can he do it?

V VOCABULARY

environment

the natural world

nervous

anxious, agitated, worried

conservation

protection of the natural environment

webmaster

a person who maintains a website

erratically

moving or behaving in a way that is not usual or predictable

≡ READ

NOTES

1   Bryan sat in science class. "Next week, we will be finishing our unit on the **environment** and **conservation**," Mrs. Jesky said. "So it's time to show what you have learned. You will complete a group project on conservation. I will be assigning each person in the group a role. Your role will help the group complete the project."

2   At once, Bryan felt his palms get damp. He told himself to breathe. He could feel his heart thumping **erratically**. *Group project? Roles?* he thought. *Anything but that.* It was like being back in sixth-grade language arts. Bryan and his group had to prepare a presentation on their book. Their teacher, Mr. Mack, gave each person a role. Bryan's role was to pick important passages from the text and explain their significance. Bryan was **nervous**. He wasn't sure how to do his task. His group asked a few times about his progress. He said he was almost done. But it was a lie. A year later, he still felt guilty for letting his group down.

3   Back in science class, Bryan tried to focus. He looked about the room tentatively. Mrs. Jesky was explaining the project. "With your group, you will be creating a Web page to explain your idea for a community conservation project. Your role will be based on what you're good at and like to do."

4   Bryan was preoccupied with the science project. Mrs. Jesky gave Bryan the role of **webmaster**. It was his job to take the group's ideas and put them into a website. *Why webmaster? Why not researcher? Why not spokesperson?* He wasn't sure he could do it. It was just like sixth-grade language arts.

5   Bryan walked slowly into science class the next day. He usually showed more energy. Mrs. Jesky noticed the change in his demeanor. "Bryan, what's wrong?" she asked.

6   "It's the project," he said. "I don't think I can do it."

7   Mrs. Jesky said, "Bryan, I gave you that role for a good reason. Those videos and presentations you are making for Ms. Reed's art club are great! You are good at presenting information in a way that people understand."

8   Bryan thought about that. Finally, he smiled. "Maybe you're right," he said. "I do really like making those videos. And people have told me they are good. Maybe I can be a good webmaster."

9   Mrs. Jesky smiled. "I know you can."

First Read

Read the story. After you read, answer the Think Questions below.

☁ THINK QUESTIONS

1. What role does Mrs. Jesky give Bryan?

   Mrs. Jesky gives Bryan _____.

2. Why did Mrs. Jesky give Bryan that role?

   She gave him that role because _____.

3. What happened to Bryan when he participated in a group project in sixth grade?

   When Bryan participated in the group project _____

   _____.

4. Use context to confirm the meaning of the word *webmaster* as it is used in "A Role to Play." Write your definition of *webmaster* here.

   Webmaster means _____.

   A context clue is _____.

5. What is another way to say that your heart is thumping *erratically*?

   Your heart is thumping _____.

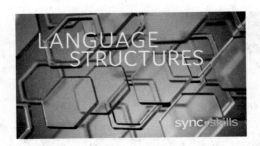

Skill:
Language Structures

★ DEFINE

In every language, there are rules that tell how to **structure** sentences. These rules define the correct order of words. In the English language, for example, a **basic** structure for sentences is subject, verb, and object. Some sentences have more **complicated** structures.

You will encounter both basic and complicated **language structures** in the classroom materials you read. Being familiar with language structures will help you better understand the text.

••• CHECKLIST FOR LANGUAGE STRUCTURES

To improve your comprehension of language structures, do the following:

✓ Monitor your understanding.

- Ask yourself: Why do I not understand this sentence? Is it because I do not understand some of the words? Or is it because I do not understand the way the words are ordered in the sentence?

✓ Break down the sentence into its parts.

✓ Confirm your understanding with a peer or teacher.

✓ In English, adjectives almost always come before the noun. Example: *He had a **big dog**.*

- A **noun** names a person, place, thing, or idea.

- An **adjective** modifies, or describes, a noun or a pronoun

- If there is more than one adjective, they usually appear in the following order separated by a comma: quantity or number, quality or opinion, size, age, shape, color. Example: *He had a **big, brown dog**.*

- If there is more than one adjective from the same category, include the word *"and."* Example: *He had a **brown and white dog**.*

✓ Ask yourself: What are the nouns in this sentence? What adjectives describe them? In what order are the nouns and adjectives?

↻ YOUR TURN

Read each sentence in the first column. Then complete the chart by writing the words and phrases into the "Adjective" and "Noun" columns. The first row has been done as an example.

Sentence	Adjective	Noun
You will complete a group project on conservation.	group	project
Bryan's role was to pick important passages from the text and explain their significance.		
His group asked a few times about his progress.		
Back in science class, Bryan tried to focus.		
Bryan, I gave you that role for a good reason.		

Skill: Drawing Inferences and Conclusions

★ DEFINE

Making **inferences** means connecting your experiences with what you read. Authors do not always tell readers directly everything that takes place in a story or text. You need to use clues to infer, or make a guess, about what is happening. To make an inference, first find facts, details, and examples in the text. Then think about what you already know. Combine the **textual evidence** with your **prior knowledge** to draw a **conclusion** about what the author is trying to communicate.

Making inferences and drawing conclusions can help you better understand what you are reading. It may also help you search for and find the author's message in the text.

••• CHECKLIST FOR DRAWING INFERENCES AND CONCLUSIONS

In order to make inferences and draw conclusions, do the following:

✓ Look for information that is missing from the text or that is not directly stated.

- Ask yourself: What is confusing? What is missing?

✓ Think about what you already know about the topic.

- Ask yourself: Have I had a similar experience in my life? Have I learned about this subject in another class?

✓ Combine clues from the text with prior knowledge to make an inference and draw a conclusion.

- Think: I can conclude _____, because the text says _____ and I know that _____.

✓ Use textual evidence to support your inference and make sure that it is valid.

Please note that excerpts and passages in the StudySync® library and this workbook are intended as touchstones to generate interest in an author's work. The excerpts and passages do not substitute for the reading of entire texts, and StudySync® strongly recommends that students seek out and purchase the whole literary or informational work in order to experience it as the author intended. Links to online resellers are available in our digital library. In addition, complete works may be ordered through an authorized reseller by filling out and returning to StudySync® the order form enclosed in this workbook.

Reading & Writing Companion   **133**

⟳ YOUR TURN

Read the following excerpt from "A Role to Play." Then, complete the multiple-choice questions below.

---

from "A Role to Play"

Back in science class, Bryan tried to focus. He looked about the room tentatively. Mrs. Jesky was explaining the project. "With your group, you will be creating a Web page to explain your idea for a community conservation project. Your role will be based on what you're good at and like to do."

Bryan was preoccupied with the science project. Mrs. Jesky gave Bryan the role of webmaster. It was his job to take the group's ideas and put them into a website. *Why webmaster? Why not researcher? Why not spokesperson?* He wasn't sure he could do it. It was just like sixth-grade language arts.

---

1. At the beginning of this excerpt, Bryan feels:

   ○ A. embarrassed by his lack of talent
   ○ B. anxious and unable to concentrate
   ○ C. angry at his teacher and classmates
   ○ D. frightened by the events in the room

2. A detail that best supports this conclusion is:

   ○ A. "tried to focus"
   ○ B. "Mrs. Jesky was explaining"
   ○ C. "With your group"
   ○ D. "what you're good at"

3. At the end of the excerpt, Bryan wonders whether:

   ○ A. Mrs. Jesky will let him quit
   ○ B. he belongs in a different class
   ○ C. other students are laughing at him
   ○ D. another role would suit him better

4. A detail that best supports this conclusion is:

   ○ A. "preoccupied with the science project"
   ○ B. "take the group's ideas"
   ○ C. *"Why not researcher?"*
   ○ D. "like sixth-grade language arts"

Close Read

✏ WRITE

LITERARY ANALYSIS: Why is Bryan nervous? How does the author show that something in his past is worrying him now? Write a short paragraph explaining why Bryan is nervous about working on a class project. Support your writing with evidence and specific details from the text, along with your personal experience. Pay attention to matching pronouns and antecedents as you write.

Use the checklist below to guide you as you write.

☐ How does Bryan feel?

☐ How do you know?

☐ Why does Bryan feel this way?

☐ How do you know?

Use the sentence frames to organize and write your literary analysis.

I believe that Bryan feels _____

because _____.

The passage supports my conclusion about _____

by telling about _____.

PHOTO/IMAGE CREDITS:

studysync®

Text Fulfillment
Through StudySync

If you are interested in specific titles, please fill out the form below and we will check availability through our partners.

ORDER DETAILS

Date:

TITLE	AUTHOR	Paperback/ Hardcover	Specific Edition *If Applicable*	Quantity

SHIPPING INFORMATION

Contact:

Title:

School/District:

Address Line 1:

Address Line 2:

Zip or Postal Code:

Phone:

Mobile:

Email:

BILLING INFORMATION   ☐ *SAME AS SHIPPING*

Contact:

Title:

School/District:

Address Line 1:

Address Line 2:

Zip or Postal Code:

Phone:

Mobile:

Email:

PAYMENT INFORMATION

☐ CREDIT CARD

Name on Card:

Card Number:

Expiration Date:

Security Code:

☐ PO

Purchase Order Number:

StudySync Text Fulfillment, BookheadEd Learning, LLC
610 Daniel Young Drive | Sonoma, CA 95476